D1172548

"*The Pummeled Heart* is not just a good book by a skilled writer, but a great book by an accomplished author and spiritual guide. It's not just a book to read, but a wonderful gift from her heart. Antoinette Bosco shares the strength, peace, and wisdom gained from her experiences of pain and tragedy.

"This is a book for all of us who must try to make sense of the dark side of life. But equally important, it is a book for professionals: counselors, ministers, psychologists, spiritual directors, anyone in a position to help people work through the days and nights when life no longer seems worth living. Keep several copies on hand to give away."

Mitch Finley
Author, *Everybody Has a Guardian Angel*

"I am delighted to recommend *The Pummeled Heart,* Antoinette Bosco's gripping account of her personal spiritual journey toward God through disappointment, pain, loss, and struggle. As a person who has also undergone the tragedy of losing a child, I have been inspired by her in my personal as well as professional life."

Raymond A. Moody, M.D., Ph.D.
Author, *Reunions* and *Life After Life*

"I began to read *The Pummeled Heart* from the standpoint of a professional seeking to help individuals in pain. From the first pages on, I was aghast at the pain Antoinette Bosco has experienced in her life, and amazed at how relevant her insights are for my own spiritual journey. I recommend the book on both grounds."

Margot Hover, D.Min.
Author, *Caring for Yourself When Caring for Others*

"Antoinette Bosco's account of her pummeled heart is far more than a record of her inexorable sufferings; it is a journey from childlike romanticism to strong, mature Christian faith. Her great gift is not merely sharing her pain and that of many others, but in showing us how we can cope with our own inevitable pain and losses. This is the most practical 'Guide to Peace' since Merton's *Seeds of Contemplation*."

A.W. Richard Sipe
Author, *A Secret World: Sexuality and the Search for Celibacy*

"Antoinette Bosco has written an extraordinary book. No one is ever going to solve completely the mystery of suffering, but in this vale of tears there are helps and graces to support and heal us on our journey. *The Pummeled Heart* is such a grace. Antoinette Bosco provides many insights into the experience of pain. Her book is a testament to the strength of the human spirit."

Rev. Robert E. Lauder, Ph.D.
Professor of Philosophy, St. John's University

"*The Pummeled Heart*, written with grace, will certainly find a home in the hearts of a wide range of readers. It offers an abundance of spiritual wisdom gathered from the crucible of the author's own personal and professional experiences. It is a beacon for the person searching for spiritual maturity and healing while taking full responsibility for his or her own faith. *The Pummeled Heart* is a grace-filled companion for the spiritual quest to 'grow strong at the broken places.'"

Richard Irwin Abrams
President, Abrams & Company Publishers, Inc.

"Antoinette Bosco draws from a broad range of spiritual sources, including many familiar though surprising names. She conveys to us that we are not alone in our trials, and that it is important to ask the questions raised by our pain, which may lead us to courage and peace."

Chuck Meyer
Author, *Surviving Death:
A Practical Guide to Caring for the Dying and Bereaved*

Antoinette Bosco

The
PuMMELED
Heart

Finding Peace Through Pain

TWENTY-THIRD PUBLICATIONS
Mystic, Connecticut 06355

Twenty-Third Publications
185 Willow Street
P.O. Box 180
Mystic, CT 06355
(203) 536-2611
800-321-0411

© Copyright 1994 Antoinette Bosco. All rights reserved. No
part of this publication may be reproduced in any manner
without prior written permission of the publisher. Write to
Permissions Editor.

ISBN 0-89622-584-4 (paper)
ISBN 0-89622-595-x (cloth)
Library of Congress Catalog Card Number 93-61500

DEDICATION

To my sons, Peter and John, and my daughter-in-law, Nancy—
who lived a relatively brief time on this earth,
but who gave us such love during their time here
that it endures, sustaining and nourishing us,
easing our pain from their physical departure.
They were, and shall always be,
as the Lord gave me to understand,
my "permanent gifts."

ACKNOWLEDGMENTS

From an early age I used to pray to the Lord that I would always be able to find the "place of refreshment, light and peace" that I believed was promised to us if only we asked. And then one day, when I was older, in my 30s, after a particularly distressing time in my life, I realized that help and refreshment and light and peace were always around the corner for me. Only it was never a *place* I would find. It was always a *person*.

Some of these "persons" became the inspiration for the learning I gained, for the wisdom I so painfully and humbly and gratefully acquired. I cannot name them all, for that would be something of a book in itself. But I want to acknowledge them—the relatives, the friends, the teachers, the co-workers, the difficult ones, the loving ones, the children, the nuns, the priests, the readers of my writings, and all the others who touched my life, whether with a caress or a sword. I acknowledge all of you, with abiding gratitude and love.

Some of the passages in this book may have a familiar ring to people who may have read some of my previous newspaper pieces. A few segments are from columns written in the past twenty years for the national Catholic News Service in Washington, D.C. It has been my privilege to be a syndicated columnist for CNS since 1974. Brief passages have also been taken from features written for *The Litchfield County Times* in Connecticut, where I have been executive editor since the founding of this newspaper in 1981.

If there is one person I would especially acknowledge by name it is Neil Kluepfel, publisher of Twenty-Third Publications. He has affirmed my writing for some twenty years, ever since I first met him and wrote articles for the magazine he founded, *Today's Parish*. In 1977, he greatly honored me by accepting my manuscript on single parenting and publishing it as *Successful Single Parenting*. Now he has again honored me by publishing *The Pummeled Heart*. No one could ask to meet and work for a finer gentleman or a more accomplished professional.

I would also give a special thanks to my children who are still with me: Sterling, Paul, Mary, Margaret, and Francis Xavier. They and their spouses and children are my circle of love and joy. I am ever grateful to God—and to them—for the blessing they are and have always been in my life.

CONTENTS

INTRODUCTION

I think now when I look back over my life that I was what one might call an odd kid. From a very early age, I had been taught that there was a God and a whole universe of sainted people in a place called heaven—and I became utterly fascinated with the idea that I was linked somehow to an extraordinary, unseen world.

I spent my elementary school years—in Catholic school, of course—reading the lives of the saints and mythology, and my teen years reading the church fathers, Thomas Aquinas, and the mystics. At times I think I had one foot in this world and one in the next (outer space, my mother might have said). Not only was I running to church a lot to stare at the stained glass windows and say Hail Marys before the sanctuary light—which noted the ever-present Blessed Sacrament—I wanted to do more for God. I wanted to be noble in suffering like the holy saints and martyrs.

I even tried to rush this when I was nine and had read the life of Blessed Kateri Tekakwitha, the Indian maiden converted by missionary priests who came to America from France in the 1600s. As one proof of her love for God, Kateri carved a cross on her leg.

I tried to do the same. Not quite as noble as she, I didn't use a sharpened knife; I only used a big needle. My mother came upon me as I was carving. Becoming immediately quite hysterical, she screamed at me that I was going to give myself blood poisoning, and she roundly punished me for my attempted excursion into sanctity. I hoped the Lord was watching to see what pain I would endure for him!

As the years went by and I continued to read this genre of spiritual literature, I came to realize, without expressing it in so many words, that I was on a crucial search. Was there really a God? Was there a point to this life, which seemed to be despised by the saints and the mystics, or at least I read it that way in my youth. For them, life seemed so often a "vale of tears," and always a cross to be borne; again, that's how I read it back then.

I remember writing down the words of St. Gregory so I could use them for meditation. I had plenty of time for meditation because I went to daily Mass from the time I was seven until I was married at age 19. "So the grape is crushed underfoot and becomes wine," wrote Gregory, "so the olive is pressed and...leaving behind its dregs, becomes rich oil....The more the fire of tribulation rids us of our rust, the cleaner will we be when we come before Christ."

Gregory's message, like so many others I read from the saints I so loved, was uncompromising. The way to heaven is rough and rocky. We have to earn that high place by more than the sweat of our brow. While I was young and untested, I had no problem with this. I loved the romanticism of suffering for the love of God. After all, I was willing to carve a cross on my leg with a needle!

But as life went on real pain set in. I had to face my mother's nervous breakdowns, so many closed doors because I was poor and female, a psychologically impaired husband and a failed marriage, the responsibility of raising and supporting six of my seven children alone, and a young brother with a fatal illness. My romanticism about pain suffered out of love for God disappeared. I wanted some answers. I didn't like the hard path. I screamed at times: Why? Why me again? What do you want of me anyway? I struggled with resentment as I still hung on to the Lord with dear might, and called this faith.

I guess it was. Certainly, I could relate to Jesus, who asked his Father, "Why have you abandoned me?" Should I be more privileged than God's Son? And I was willing to try to understand that when Jesus said the "seed must die" so that new life can be born, he meant it. Is death ever painless? And what is the "seed" if not our self-centeredness, anger, unfairness to others, hardness, the attractiveness of sowing discord when it means advancing our position at the expense of another, and so on. Surely the "seed" of self has to die, or we never gain the new life Jesus holds out to us. How else can selfishness die but through having it beaten out of us, as Gregory put it, so that our hearts can soften enough to feel compassion and love for others, and a yearning for the Source of this love? Even my notes from Gregory affirmed that "Renouncing what we have is not so much; renouncing what we are amounts to a great deal." Indeed, it's the ticket to heaven.

And so my acceptance of God's mysterious ways of sending us pain and discomfort as a way of freeing us from the immobility of remaining a "seed," was a happy choice. Yet, as my faith foundation became firm, I learned that I hadn't "made it," as we like to put it. In fact, as the blows kept coming (and some were so hard I sometimes felt like Job reincarnated!), I often tried to console myself philosophically, to keep my eye on the "prize," which is heaven. I took to quoting people like C.S. Lewis who recognized that we live, after all, in a "shadowland," for earth is "not our permanent home."

But as the decade of the 90s began, I faced new traumas that had me asking God again: What is it you're asking of me? Where are you taking me? When is enough enough?

In one year's time I had blows that were a kind of spiritual endurance contest. My oldest son, born with extreme myopia, experienced cranial pressure that forced a blood vessel to burst in the retina of his left eye, leaving him effectively blind in that eye. Now he is at risk of the same thing happening to his remaining eye. Then two of my grandchildren, at ages 2 and 4, were in a near fatal auto crash. My son Sterling, adopted by us in 1951 when he was 15, suffered three heart attacks. And my youngest, Peter, the child I called the light of my life, left this world at age 27.

For ten years I had known that Peter was in trouble. He had had an onslaught of illness when he was 17, being hit with one of those mentally destroying maladies that come under the umbrella of "bipolar affective disorders." I was told by one of his doctors when he left a suicide note at 17 that his illness was permanent and that he would spend most of his life hospitalized.

Neither Peter nor I accepted that. With good medical care, determination to seek health, and much prayer, he got on with his life, completing a two-year commitment in the U.S. Army, finishing college with honors and a teaching degree, teaching mathematics in a Catholic school in Guam, and even writing books.

But he didn't heal; he suffered with ever-increasing pain from being, in his words "incomplete....My life is like a Rolls Royce without sparkplugs. It looks great, but it has a hidden flaw that keeps it from running properly," he said in a 90-minute farewell tape he left, addressing us with sadness in his voice as "Dear Family."

We didn't know how despairing life had become for Peter. He did everything possible to keep us from knowing he had made a choice that would bring us great sorrow. In his own words, it was time for him to "go home." On March 18, 1991, he walked to a pond about a mile from home, where he used to go to meditate, and put a bullet through his head.

At first I thought I would die, too. I never believed I could survive the death of one of my children. I would lie in bed at night and my body would take over, with what felt like labor pains. From some depth, I was trying to give birth to Peter again.

But somewhere I found strength, I believe from all the prayers that others were saying for us. And then there were the unexplainable ways that Peter stayed in touch with me, so that I never ever could doubt that life goes on. I knew he was happy and I began to find peace.

Then two years later came the most crushing blow of all, the unbelievable, horrifying news that my son John, 41, and his beautiful wife, Nancy Renee, 32, had been found murdered in their bed in their Bigfork, Montana, home. This was beyond belief. How could there be such evil in this world? How could two fine people—a cabinet maker who played the violin, and his wife who came from a South Dakota farm and loved poetry—be blown away by an armed intruder invading the sanctity of their home!

Suicide, which I had been forced to face, was unbelievable pain. For the survivors, it is tormenting and almost unbearable. You cannot put it out of your mind that maybe, just maybe, it could have been prevented. Yet, with suicide, there is the reality of choice, that someone in a desperate condition chooses to end their pain. And so it has a kind of closure to it that keeps it a private and very personal act. If the survivors can accept that, they can come to peace.

But murder is different. Murder shatters the peace of

one's life. For murder is the entrance of the worst evil imaginable into your home, into all the safe places of your life, forever blasting any illusions you might have had that good can protect you from evil. Evil is real and never again can I question its power.

After that horrible news—John and Nancy were killed on August 12, 1993—I used to look at my mother-ring. My six birth children had it made for me one year as a birthday present. My stone, the September sapphire, is large and in the center. Nicely arranged around it are two aquamarines for my two sons, Paul and Frank, born in March; two amethysts for my two daughters, Mary and Margaret, both born in February; and two diamonds, for my two sons, John and Peter, my April babies. I would stare at the ring and reflect on how my two diamonds are somewhere in the heavens where they belong, with their Maker.

On the Sunday after I got the news of the murders, I was at Mass, kneeling, asking God for understanding, yet thanking God for my two sons, who were my gifts, even though they were only temporary gifts. As I silently uttered those last words, I felt myself struck, almost as if I had been slapped, and I distinctly heard the words, "They are a permanent gift." A priest friend to whom I related the incident said, simply, "You were corrected." I found myself smiling, and I was soaring because I could smile again.

I learned then that while I felt somewhat defeated by life, my faith would come to my assistance. It was as if I heard the Lord remind me that along with the blows, there are also joys. And that was true. For, along with the dark side, there were the bright moments. My grandchildren survived and are doing well; my daughter Mary gave birth to a gorgeous baby girl, naming her Sophia Celeste Antoinette ("heavenly wisdom," and her grandmother's namesake!); my son Frank's wife, Judi, also gave birth to a gorgeous baby girl, Talia Joella; my son Peter's books—he wrote three of them in the last year and a half of his life—were all published posthumously by major publishers, his legacy to us and others; my adopted son Sterling, with a machine in his chest to shock his heart and get it regulated is doing well; my 85-year-old mother has come back from a paralysis and is walking again.

Those three years became a time for reflecting on how life is full of the bad and the good, the trials and the triumphs. It was a period plunging me back into the paradox all Christians face—Is this, Lord, how you force us to stay on the right path, the one that leads to the destiny you set for us, that place where our hearts and souls are merged with the Source of our being?

I think sometimes that I was given a glimpse of this pattern that God has designed for me when I was at the impressionable age of 16. It was in a dream.

I was at the base of a mountain and had the sudden urge to climb to the top. I sensed I would find unspeakable beauty there—and the meaning of life.

And so I climbed. But when I got to the top, all I saw was yet another mountain. And to get to the top of that one, I had to climb down into a valley before I could ascend.

When I again got to the top, it was the same.

Repeatedly, I climbed and descended until I was exhausted.

But still I wouldn't stop. Something urged me forward.

Finally, after climbing innumerable mountains, I descended to a valley, and before me, in the base of yet another mountain, was a cave. A bright light illuminated it. I ran to the entrance, and there, in radiance, was the Blessed Mary with her Babe.

She handed the child to me and to this day I remember the overwhelming sense of the blending of myself with the Child Jesus, and the ecstasy of joy I felt in that moment.

I awoke, still dazed by the prize.

In later years, it struck me that in my dream I had found the fullness of my life not at the top of the mountain, but in the valley. Was that to be a metaphor for my life? I don't know. What I do know is that life has been that dream—the mountains and the valleys, the anticipation of glory and the reality of gloom. And yet, when I have been closest to God are the times when I have been immersed in the gloom and asking why.

For it is then that my heart, pummeled in pain, softens—and I am lost in the Mystery that torments me and consoles me at the same time. Not knowing for sure, the belief still comes from my melted heart that I will one day again know—but this time in fullness, not in a dream—the joy of being one with the Child.

I do not know the future, no one does. I don't know what God still has in store for me because, as the poster so brightly puts it, "Be patient with me because God isn't finished with me yet." But I do know with unshakable faith that if hard times return, the pain is not impotent. For God gets closer—blow by blow—and mysteriously yet truly, these blows are really God's wake up calls—fitting us for eternity.

CHAPTER ONE

LIFE SPARES NO ONE FROM THE BLOWS

My Aunt Justina always used to say, "It's a great life if you don't weaken." I grew up listening to that observation—and grew older trying to face its truth.

Look at anyone, and rarely do you find a life story journey that has been consistently smooth, uncomplicated, and free of discomfort. There are always unexpected setbacks, disillusionments, near defeats, and incalculable pain. We struggle to survive the blows and to accept the losses like divorce, incapacitating illness, unemployment, death of loved ones, and the passage of youth—though they can send us close to despair.

In my younger days, when the unexpected blows came my way, I would look to the church for answers, or, if not answers at least solace. I would be told over and over that the suffering we must endure is "God's will." Repeatedly I would go back to my private pain bent over, trying to obey the advice that I had been given, that I had to "carry my cross." I remember one priest telling me, I think in jest, that "there's nothing wrong with pain, except that it hurts." Unfortunately, I couldn't start laughing until the bleeding stopped.

I truly believed that these people of God who told me to carry my cross and bear my human pains with dignity and faith—preaching that these had a purifying purpose in my journey to heaven—were being absolutely honest. They probably believed they were being empathetic, for surely there was truth in what they advised. None of us is strengthened humanly or spiritually by the easy life. We need the blows of setbacks, loneliness, and loss to lead us out of the self-centeredness that blocks us from extending our hand to God. The poet Oscar Wilde put it bluntly: "How else but through a broken heart can the good Lord enter in?"

The late Bishop Fulton J. Sheen, on his famed television show of the 50s and in his books, often used vivid images to help us understand the necessity of troubles. Only after the marble is cut and chiseled and pounded and polished does it turn into a Pietà, he would say in his inimitable way, giving us a metaphor for why we had to endure pain.

Yet for most of us, getting to the point of being able to understand advice like "carrying your cross" and "there's nothing wrong with pain except that it hurts," or even the poetic gems of Wilde and Sheen, is a journey couched in mystery.

This is not surprising, because all these insights, valid as they are, are somehow incomplete. They tell us what to endure and they praise the good that may come from our poundings, but they don't tell us why. Why does pain have to be the path to God?

In my own personal struggles I often think of the lines from the haunting song of "Gethsemane," from the musical "Jesus Christ Superstar." There Jesus poignantly and assertedly confronts his Father, saying, "Why should I die? Can you show me now that I would not be killed in vain? ...Show me there's a reason for your wanting me to die. You're far too keen on where and how and not so hot on why...."

That seems to be our fate, too, not really understanding why we have to bend so often, and so unexpectedly, to the blows. And frankly, I don't think we're ever going to really know why there's so much suffering individually and in the world. Theologians have spent centuries trying to explain the problem of evil, and still the answers remain elusive.

Our late great pontiff, Pope John XXIII, acknowledged this in his wonderful autobiography *Journal of a Soul*. He wrote, "Above all, one must always be ready for the Lord's surprise moves, for though he treats his loved ones well, he generally likes to test them with all sorts of trials, such as bodily infirmities, bitterness of soul, and sometimes opposition so powerful as to transform and wear out the life of the servant of the servants of God, making it a real martyrdom...."

This testing, in truth, becomes our greatest challenge. Some make it and some don't. As writer John

Steinbeck wrote in his *The Acts of King Arthur and His Noble Knights*, "Somewhere in the world there is defeat for everyone. Some are destroyed by defeat, and some made small and mean by victory. Greatness lives in one who triumphs equally over defeat and victory."

That is wisdom, but it still leaves unanswered: How does one get to that "greatness?"

I don't think it comes from trying to conform to simplistic advice like "carry your cross." That passive, defeating acceptance doesn't work any more, and for good reason. It's out of context. It doesn't say enough or help enough because we're complex, thinking human beings, beset with all kinds of needs—physical, emotional, psychological, and spiritual—and we've got to find help that nourishes us in all these areas or we become, in effect, disabled.

When the blows come, we have to know what we're dealing with, and the major, though often denied, truth is that we are angry, sometimes rip-roaring angry. If we don't acknowledge that anger, it goes underground, settling pathologically inside a person, becoming depression. It's not the loss of a job, the death of a child, a divorce, growing old, etc., but the internal anger-reaction to these, which causes a person to become depressed.

I can talk about the disabling condition of depression and empathize with someone suffering from this state because I briefly fell into that abyss when I was trying to passively carry my cross after my marriage failed and I was left to raise and support six children.

The trauma of depression is devastating. You become immobilized, unable to make decisions, uninterested, and unable to care about anything. You become terrorized because you are unable to communicate and unbearably lonely because you are not able to connect to other human beings. You become a frustration to friends and relatives who alternately empathize and criticize. They tell you to look up and see the sun and the trees. They don't know that for the person who has lost hope, albeit temporarily, there is no sun, there are no trees. To be immobilized, detached, terrorized, hopeless, and isolated is what Percy Knauth, after his long bout with depression, described as *A Season in Hell.*

Even the poet Dante had that concept of hell. In his *Inferno* he leads his readers through the dark regions of hell with this warning overhanging the entrance: "Abandon hope all ye who enter here." As he unfolds the stories of the tragic, doomed figures, you proceed with him deeper and deeper into the regions of hell, where the sins become ever more heinous. Finally, when you go with him to the innermost regions of hell—where Satan is—how do we find the Prince of Darkness: He is immobilized, frozen—encased in ice—in eternal isolation, in hell.

When the reaction to the blows of life is serious depression, it takes something close to a miracle to help melt the ice and get unstuck so as to go on with life, with hope, and finding joy again. But it can be done, and once you are in the light again, life takes on a beauty you couldn't have imagined before.

When I think of the many times I have had to deal with pain and tragedy, I am also conscious of what I was supposed to learn from these shocks. Simply put, it is how to discern what is really important. And as for what really matters, I have learned it is only life and death.

Imagine, for example, if your child is in danger of death—and I have lost two sons—how little such things as furniture, a clean house, a job promotion, or a cranky relative matter. You become terribly conscious of how finite this world is and you reach out for what is lasting, the Eternal. You go to God.

I have learned that pain is an activator. Because of it I have grown as a person, and as a lover of Christ. This happened because I learned it isn't enough to passively carry a cross. You have to pick it up, fight with it, deal with its weight by lifting it over your head, and, from the muscles you develop by dealing with your cross, finally, peculiarly, you know that you can now love it.

I am often reminded of a line from Hemingway's *A Farewell to Arms,* that "life breaks us all, and afterward many are strong at the broken places." I wonder...perhaps that's because they have learned not to carry their cross but to exercise with it.

CHAPTER TWO

THE HURTING IS FOR REAL

Was Hemingway right? Does the world break all of us? I don't know for sure, but talk to friends, neighbors, co-workers, family members, and read the daily papers. You certainly get the idea that it does. Meet some of my friends....

Sue was a young wife from Brooklyn, New York, married for five years when her husband developed a strange heart infection. He had had a heart condition and an operation in his youth, so he was too vulnerable to lick this infection. He died, leaving her a widow in her late 20s.

Debra's husband was a state trooper in Connecticut. On Thanksgiving day a few years ago, he was felled by a hit and run driver. Debra was left with three small children to raise. Exactly one year later, on the next Thanksgiving day, her beloved father died.

Ben was in the prime of his life, age 48 and in good health, or so he thought. An interior designer, he was in his Manhattan office when he suddenly fell to the floor. He had had a stroke and would be in a wheel-chair for the rest of his life.

Jason, 15 years old, was at a school football practice when he was hit and knocked down; his head protected by his gear, or so it seemed. He went home, had supper, went to take a shower, and screamed from a searing pain in his head. His parents rushed him to the emergency room. The diagnosis was bad. He had a ruptured blood vessel in his head. For days it was touch and go, but fortunately, he survived. He will have some paralysis, but he has his life.

The daily newspapers report volumes of tragic tales about people who encounter murder, sex abuse, mutilation from accidents, muggings, and other horrors. Then there are people who have terrible torments visited upon them, not physically, but heartbreakingly— like learning that a son or daughter is on drugs, or that they have taken a few drinks, gotten into a car, and killed someone.

In an inspiring book called *Seek Treasures in Small Fields,* Sister Joan Puls shares the story of her personal blow, a descent into mental illness, one of the most defeating crosses one can confront. "The most remote thought in my mind when I was thirty was the possibility of finding myself incarcerated in a mental hospital, deprived even of the necklace-cross that was part of my religious habit (I might use it as a weapon against myself), an object of pity and grave concern to family and community," she writes.

"My Ph.D. was still fresh in my possession. My students were avid and devoted. My life extended before me, a career in teaching, partnership with colleagues who had once taught me. How did I know that God was about to 'break in' precisely where I felt strong and invulnerable, my mental and emotional stability? And that is what happened...."

Sister Joan, a Franciscan, well describes the bleakness she had to contend with. "It was the onset of a mysterious numbness that crept into my whole being, caused me to want to die, closed down all my connections with the basic ingredients of life: color, activity, conversation, relationships.

"I could not feel the wind on my face, the hand that clasped mine, my sister's death from cancer, the ground under my feet, the meaning of anything I heard or read. I was alone in my deep dark tunnel and there was no end to it, it seemed. I simply sat there— mute, pitiable, wasted."

In this beautifully honest and revealing book, Sister Joan tells of her personal journey back to health and what she learned from her pain. She summarizes it this way: "All of life is a letting go, a rehearsal for the final grand performance. We die many times over, through loss and disappointment. The deprivation is startling and acute. The promise of resurrection is vague and often unconvincing. But we learn, in painful stages, that new life does issue from darkness and death."

Not everyone, of course, deals with such heavy blows. For many, the lesser blows seem to accumulate to the point where they are really defeated. Don't these people need empathy and help, too? Definitely. When it comes to hurting, we've got to recognize that this is a qualitative, not quantitative, problem.

As an example, a woman friend was depressed and upset one day recently. She and her family had awakened to a cold house, no heat and no hot water. Showers had to be put off and everyone shivered as they tried to get ready for their day at work and school. To make matters worse, the phone line to her oil company was out of order, so she wasn't even able to put in a distress call for repairs.

Underneath all the annoyance was a different worry, a real fear. Both her children had been ill the week before, one with flu and one with mononucleosis, still uncured, and a cold house was not the place for either of them to be. "I've had enough," she complained; "why can't things be easier?"

I will never know the answer to that question. What I do know is that in real life difficult things are going to happen to us no matter how much we try to prevent them or to protect ourselves against them.

A couple of years ago my daughter Margee called me on a Saturday morning, definitely distressed. A fish tank that her husband had made for their two little boys had toppled over, spilling the water all over her new rug and, of course, killing the fish, a tragedy that had my two grandsons very upset.

I went over and helped her with the mess and her emotional blue fog. But I couldn't answer her question, "Why do miserable things like this happen?" I just know that uncomfortable, annoying, miserable, traumatic, and tragic things do happen. They are built into human existence.

Two summers ago I had my first automobile accident after more than four decades of driving, and it happened where they say most accidents happen—close to home. In fact, it was at the end of my driveway, which exits to a main road. I was putting my foot on the brake when the car suddenly lurched forward, hitting a van. My gas pedal had gotten stuck when I inadvertently kicked a small heel protector pad under the pedal.

Fortunately, neither I nor the other driver was hurt. But I felt terrible. That woman was peacefully on her way to work and I became the agent that messed up her day. Why did this have to happen? I don't know.

I remember years ago reading *A Retreat for Lay People* by Msgr. Ronald Knox in which he talked about all the inconveniences and troubles that happen to us. "Why do they occur?" he asked, and answered with another question, "Well, why shouldn't they happen?" In other words, why do we expect that life comes with some kind of guarantee that every day will go smoothly? We seem to be locked in a mode of "great expectations." Our human nature wants the self and the ego never to be put out.

Yet the self and the ego have to be jolted or we never come fully alive. That's the hard truth and the mystery. I remember about six years ago interviewing Tom Jones (not the singer, but the lyricist for the songs in the great, enduring musical *The Fantasticks*). I had always been fascinated by the wisdom in his prize-winning song, "Try to Remember," especially the line that says, "Without a hurt, the heart is hollow." He told me that he had learned this truth from his own pain, and he also said that "without the dark side, we would never be able to appreciate the light," paraphrasing what the saints have preached down through the ages.

And so the mystery remains that we have sorrow so we can understand joy; failure, so we can recognize success; pain, so we can relish pleasure, and so on. Somehow, built into this mystery of the duality in life is a blueprint for growth that has the potential for shaping us into the people God wants us to be.

It's not the blueprint for sissies. As the priest I quoted earlier pointed out, "There's nothing wrong with pain except that it hurts." I have never found a way to contradict that. But I have learned from experience that, like lyricist Tom Jones said, the ones who come through the hurts have something great in return, no more hollow hearts.

CHAPTER THREE

THE INJUSTICE OF IT ALL

All right, so we've all been broken by life from time to time. It's a common human experience. But why? That's the big question. Why does suffering have to happen? Why are there uncomfortable, annoying, miserable, traumatic, and tragic things in our lives? Why can't things be easier?

Ah, if I knew the answer to this, I would be the greatest sage in the world. One of my younger sisters had a favorite expression which she used with various degrees of seriousness. "There's no justice in this world." If she lost a volleyball game, or cut her finger, or lost a casual boyfriend to another girl, she would invariably laugh, shrug her shoulders and say, "No justice!" Later, when she experienced a severe personal crisis, she cried bitterly "No justice" with much apparent justification.

I think we all yield to the temptation of complaining about the unfairness of life at times, especially when this comes close to home. I thought of my sister's "no justice" when I heard another woman's sad story (at a time I was going through hard times myself). The woman was in her 70s, blind since birth, and lived alone. She functioned like a sighted person, however, because she had lived in the same house all her life and knew every wall and corner in it. She cleaned and cooked and cared well for her home and herself. But now she was being forcefully evicted by a member of her family, because he said it was too expensive for her to stay in the house.

When I talked to the woman, it was clear that she couldn't bear the thought of being in new, unfamiliar surroundings. She felt that this was the end of her independence and her will to live. It was a tragic finale for her.

When I was young, Catholics would readily say that God sent suffering to those he loved most and that the "back was made for the burden." I was told that God wouldn't send us trials heavier than we could bear. This pious, if not reasonable, explanation for sorrows and tragedy merely sprinkled holy water on such situations. It also obscured the reality that some people of great faith do have physical and mental breakdowns because of their burdens. Some people, in fact, like the blind woman, are undergoing pain and blows that are downright unjust. There is often "no justice" in what humans do to one another. Such examples touch us all.

One woman I know has ten daughters, and she once also had a son. When he was eleven years old, he was playing with a friend who decided to show him his father's rifle. It went off accidentally and my friend's son was killed. God's will? I don't believe so. It was an unfortunate human tragedy and plainly "no justice."

For those people who have been victims of unjust happenings—in varying degrees of intensity—faith can understandably be strained. But once the "no justice" is spoken and faced, what then? Can people cement together the remaining pieces of their lives, and without bitterness toward God or other people, struggle to regain their wholeness?

That has always been the major question facing all of us when our faith is challenged and we waver on a tightrope, tempted to see God as the cause of our pain, we cry out for justice, rather than the hope of our healing.

Yet, difficult as it is to take, the pain of injustice can be like an internal beauty treatment. As someone wrote once: "A clay pot sitting in the sun will always be a clay pot. It has to go through the white heat of the furnace to become porcelain."

Other bonuses come our way, too, when we open ourselves to God's white heat of healing. For starters, we learn a new definition of freedom, that freedom means truly to choose our own burden. People have wondered about my life, commenting on the difficulties, the injustice of having been left with the responsibility of raising, supporting, caring for, and educating six children. And yet I chose to accept this burden. I lived the life I freely chose to live. People have asked me, too, why I never married again. I've told them, because I couldn't choose among all those men out there just dying to be number seven in my life! Examine your own lives and I wager that you will learn that you have been freely choosing your burdens much more than you realized.

We also learn as part of the healing process to move on, because we have reached a point in life where there is an unexpected unfolding of events for us. We are thrust on in life by traumatic developments that shake us, requiring us to move on. And motion is, so often, the sign of new life.

I remember a story my brother Joe told me once. It concerned a man who had come up against one of those points in life when he had to take the risk of making a change or being immobilized. He was retired, had enough money to live on, and was certainly comfortable in the eyes of the world. Yet he undertook a journey, going around the world in a boat by himself. When he returned, reporters asked him why had he risked everything when he had such a comfortable life. He answered, "Because I didn't want to live in the backyard of life."

I think some of us might relate to that. We used to call it being in a rut. Certainly it is where some of us were when we felt a major blow in our lives. I have learned from my blows that taking steps and finding the courage to get out of the backyard to begin a new phase of life, brings its own, sometimes unexpected, rewards.

I think another thing we learn from the healing process is greater understanding of our own needs and less concern about the way others will judge how we live our lives. This doesn't mean we should get complacent, however. Even if today has become bright again, we can never be certain about tomorrow and the pitfalls it might bring. The greatest mistake any of us can make is to think "I've made it." This would be a dangerous self-deception because to be alive means to constantly face change, new situations, and unexpected mishaps, as well as personal growth which brings us into new places where we don't know ourselves any more and we must confront this new stranger. This happens especially at the points in our lives that we could clearly label "transitions," like turning 50, falling in love, having our youngest leave home, a child getting married. As author Faith Baldwin put it, "Time is a dressmaker specializing in alterations."

Another pitfall that can threaten us is what I bluntly call the periodic, temporary loss of faith. We get overcome with the dark feeling that nothing makes sense. It is a bleak place to be. But we find ourselves there now and then simply because that's life.

What has astounded me in such times is how remarkably and surprisingly God re-reveals his creative power to help us hang on to faith. One of the strangest places I ever found God unexpectedly communicating with me was at a biology lecture some dozen years ago. A brilliant biologist, Dr. Bentley Glass, was speaking about the origins of life. He said that if all the sperm that resulted in the birth of the three to four billion people on this earth could be collected, they would fit into a four-ounce container. And if all the eggs were similarly collected, these would fill a one and a half pint container. In other words, all the life-beginnings and all the coding that determines everything about a person, from the color of eyes to personality, for all the people now in this universe, could fit into a glass and a half. Truly, God holds the whole world in his hands—and that's you and me, sisters and brothers.

In the face of that Mystery, I feel the immensity of my own importance that I was selected for life—and a destiny that was described by Jesus as one that eyes haven't seen and ears haven't heard, it is so great. And I have been able more and more as the years go on to hold on to my faith and cherish it, knowing that God will be revealed again to me when I need it most and in the most unexpected ways—like a lecture on biology.

CHAPTER FOUR

WE EXPECT TOO MUCH

Once in a while you have a week that makes you wonder if there is, indeed, something to the popular belief that the stars are temporarily roughing you up. I had one not long ago. For starters, I had gone to a memorial service for a 92-year-old woman, a longtime dear friend. The family had arranged a musical tribute to her and the concert was in a building that had been an old grange hall, with parking on the adjacent grass field.

I was one of the last to leave and when I got to my car, I found it with the back fender half on the ground and considerable damage to the rear left body. It was a classic case of hit-and-run and I was left to pick up the pieces—literally.

Naturally, I felt abused. For a few minutes, I was downright angry with the thought of all the trouble this was going to cost me. For I now faced a complete change in my work schedule, with a lot of time lost as I made a police report, got my car to a garage, rented another car, and waited for repairs to be completed. I was close to having a tantrum until I began to look on the bright side. And there was a decided positive side, specifically that I hadn't been in the car and wasn't hurt.

That week I had also put a lot of energy and hope into being able to hire a co-worker, someone who had once worked for me and was a capable and lovely person. She had been through a lot of change in the previous two years: a marriage break-up, making child-care arrangements, and taking on a new job in public relations. The idea of coming back to journalism appealed to her, and I made her a good offer.

But in the end, she declined. I could understand. Her life had been disrupted enough and it was difficult for her to contemplate another change so soon. And so, I was back to square one in my search for a good worker.

Then, a key co-worker came back from vacation on crutches, with a bone fracture in his foot from playing basketball. He was in too much pain to put in the required hours at work and so I had to work almost double time to make up for what he was unable to do.

At one point, I was in a near frenzy with deadline pressure and so I ran out in the pouring rain to grab a bite of lunch. The office driveway was wet and slippery, and, not being careful, I fell, doing damage to both my knees.

Well, it went on like that. A friend who's into astrology told me something about Pluto entering one of my "houses," whatever that means, and she warned me I was in for a rough ride for the next six months. "Find a solid stake and hang on tight," she said. I answered, "Gee, thanks," and was happy I didn't believe in any of that (at least I never did!).

Since I usually fall back on a more Christ-centered approach, I put aside the "bad stars" theory and thought about life. It occurred to me that while it's normal to be upset over mishaps, most of the time our reactions are exaggerated for a rather human reason. It's because our expectations have been messed with.

I had the expectation that I'd leave the memorial service and have a peaceful, productive day; that my former co-worker would take the job and make my life a lot easier; that my present co-worker would come back healthy and refreshed from his vacation; that I'd go out and get lunch without injuring myself.

For some reason we go through life with daily expectations that all will be well, and guess what? It often isn't. For those times when the smooth ride gets bumpy, or downright destructive, we have to adjust our expectations, realistically accepting the fact that life comes packaged in light and dark.

I have learned this, small bits at a time, from experiences that range from merely uncomfortable to downright tragic. And yet, when I remember these incidences, it occurs to me that I have always, and sometimes immediately, been given something I call "grace" to help me see the beauty that lies beyond the beast.

I remember a morning some twenty years ago when my son Peter's school schedule was changed because of required testing, and bus service was not available.

It was a freezing winter day and far too cold for Peter to ride a bike the eight miles to school. The only thing that made sense for me was to interrupt my work day—I was on the staff of a university—and drive him to school.

Well, it was one of those days when the boss was in a foul mood, furious that I was not going to be available at that specific time. That put me in a dark mood, too. By the time I got back to the campus after taking Peter to school, I couldn't find a parking space. I ended up a mile away in a far lot. I was hungry since I had used up lunch time for my motherly chore. I visualized trying to eat a sandwich at my desk, pen in hand, phone ringing, boss growling. The walk to my building was very long in icy weather and I was freezing. All in all, my mood was lousy; I was in a self-centered, petulant condition, feeling very abused.

Unexpectedly, as I was walking along briskly the sun came out and the wind disappeared. The change took me by surprise and I slowed down. Immediately the air felt crisp and wonderful. I took a deep breath, remembering what my mother had so often told me— that breathing God's fresh air is the way we house-clean our bodies, cleansing them, taking away the impurities. I smiled, as I always do when I remember my mother's creative myths.

With that smile, my whole mood followed suit. Why in heaven's name had I been sour, feeling sorry for myself? In asking that question, the answer was suddenly very clear. I was feeling sorry for myself because I had been looking at the transportation chore from

the perspective of inconvenience and discomfort because of how it had disrupted my schedule. If I had,
instead, looked at that chore from the perspective of
my good fortune at being able to do it, there's no way
on earth I would have been annoyed.

The fact is, I was fortunate to have a body that func-
tions on its own power, moving without pain; to have
a car that had gas, started up, and moved us to our
destination; a job to leave and go back to, which
makes it possible for us to have the house and car,
and warm coats to protect us from the wind. With a
change in my perspective about the unexpected chore
I had inherited that day, my whole being changed,
from miserable to joyful. That's what I call being
blessed, and I received the grace to see this, thanks to
God who let the sun shine on me so suddenly that
day.

Ever since that eye-opener about how easily we can
get sucked into self-pity, I've noticed there are a lot of
people walking around with a "poor me" complex,
wearing self-pity like a second skin.

There was Regina. Every sentence she uttered was
prefaced "With my luck..." and the rest of the statement was always bad news. My relative Justine had a
way of finding the flip side of all nice things. I bought
her an apron, but it was too pretty to wear. I bought
her a cake, but it was too fattening to eat. Mary was
one who never said a word. She just sighed, deep,
heavy sighs, regularly. You couldn't mistake what she
was saying about her terrible lot in life, even though
she minced words.

Self-pity happens to most of us now and then. Something triggers a disturbance inside us and all of a sudden we find our expectations jolted and we concentrate on our deprivations. That happens to me almost every time I see an Olympic skater like a fluid doll conquering the ice. It always hits me that I'll never know how it feels to glide over ice because I've never been on ice skates. I'll never learn how to swim either, because I never tested the waters until I was an adult and then I was too deathly afraid to stay in them.

This makes me remember my young days when, because of my strict Italian family, I was not allowed to leave the house for anything but school and church. I started to feel angry that I missed out on all the sporty, fun things that were a part of the world of my peers, but not mine.

One depressed thought usually leads to another, and I remember days when I would find myself looking at the house and thinking, I'll never own decent furniture; looking in the mirror and closing my eyes because I couldn't see a Cover Girl face; looking at television and resenting the fact that I'll never have a husband worrying about whether I've taken my Geritol.

I remember how that commercial—something about the power of Geritol to keep romance in a marriage, I guess—got me laughing one day. Humor made the pendulum swing back and I found myself concentrating on other, more positive, deprivations, like: I don't have cancer. I never lost a limb, I haven't been hungry since I was 19, I am not unemployed.

From my own weaknesses, I've come to understand

why some people are chronic complainers, mired in self-pity or on the greed track. It is because basic to our nature as human beings is the desire not just to have, but to have *more*. Some people suffer from a constant condition of subjective poverty. No one denies that objective poverty exists, where people have no shoes or running water, have shabby homes and scanty food. Subjective poverty is different. It is relative. It means feeling poor in relation to others, feeling deprived because we don't have what someone else has, be it money, fame, good looks, good health, and so on.

We are "poor" proportionately to our expectations of what we should have, expectations that are determined by what we observe to be goodies not only available to, but actually possessed by, others, and not by ourselves. When people start to concentrate on what they perceive as their deprivations, and don't bounce back to a balanced position by looking at all the "grace" they have been given, they readily fall into self-pity, a hideous trap.

I remember reading words of wisdom once from St. Francis de Sales, something I scribbled in a notebook back in my college days. He wrote that truly rich people are the ones who are content with their possessions, not looking over their shoulders to see how much more other people have, and then becoming miserable from the inequality. Truly the choice of being rich or "poor me" is mostly ours to make.

If we can get real about expectations, putting them aside and concentrating instead on how to make ourselves strong enough to deal with setbacks and pains, then we are advancing to maturity, which is essential for real spiritual growth. Maturity was nicely defined in a book called *The Mature Mind* by H.A. Overstreet: "To mature is to bring one's powers to realization." It doesn't take a genius to figure out that if everything in life were easy, then we'd never get to find out if we had powers, or learn how to use them, or feel the joy that comes when one becomes internally empowered. In addition, if we never got uncomfortable, we'd probably never ask for God's help, question what life means, or yearn for paradise.

Setbacks, problems, and hurts may be the dark side of the divine plan, but they are an essential challenge, maybe the only one that can get us moving out of the comfort zone that keeps us immature.

CHAPTER FIVE

MAKING SENSE OF PAIN

One thing about pain, it comes in more forms than one can imagine, in more intensity than one can explain. And sometimes it is unbearable because the person suffering the pain can't get beyond it to see purpose. Most of us can relate to that, because few of us get through even the years of our youth without having to wrestle with the question of why. Why pain, why suffering, why tragedy, why injustice, why illness, why devastating accidents, why death of the young, why the silence of God...why, why, why?

All of us have our sad stories; not all of us have a neatly wrapped up ending. Maybe that's because when it comes to trying to understand or make sense out of the painful experiences we must endure individually, or as members of the human race in a physical world—where war, rape, and starvation exist—there just aren't any neat or satisfactory explanations.

After a tragedy I lived through, the death of my

youngest son, I found myself asking over and over, "How do I make sense out of this pain?" I asked many to share their thoughts with me in seeking an answer to this question. One man I spoke to was Ram Dass, author of many spiritual books, and a popular speaker on subjects that have to do with compassion, suffering, spiritual awareness, and the interconnectedness of all life.

Ram Dass, a tall man, with a fringe of silver hair that looks almost halo-like, who carries prayer beads as do many devotees of Eastern faiths, stood straight and closed his eyes as he contemplated my question. Then he said, "Oh, but you are asking the wrong question. You can't make sense out of pain. The question you must ask is, 'How do I come to find peace out of my pain?'" And he went on, "You can only do this by walking into your grief and accepting the Mystery, knowing that He is with you."

I have carried that wisdom with me ever since. I wish I had been given this gift much earlier in my life, so I could have shared it with others, like a decade ago, when I sat with a mother whose 17-year-old son had left her a suicide note.

The agony she felt was intense, for her heart had been pierced with a sword. The note was sudden and shocking. Her son did well in school, had never given her any trouble, was liked by his friends and teachers, and had been demonstratively devoted to her. Yet this day he had written, "Dear Mom, by the time you read this, I shall be dead."

Fortunately, he was found before attempting to do

any damage to himself and his mother immediately got professional help for him. But the explanation for why he would have tried to take such a drastic and terminal step was a mindblower for her, and she was suffering, trying to make sense of it all.

Her son told her that for months he had been struggling with trying to find a reasonable explanation for why he was living, and, little by little, he sank deeper and deeper into terror. That was because, he said, he couldn't come up with an answer. He looked at his home, his school, his relationships, his schedules, his studies, his hobbies, and even his future work goals— and everything fell into a pot of uselessness. He had concluded that it didn't matter what he did. Nothing made a difference. It was all a game of doing time from birth till death, and he had concluded that it didn't make sense to play the game. He believed that suicide was a better answer once he could no longer make sense of his pain.

That was a line of pessimism I had heard several times before, when I was on the faculty of a college. I remember one young woman who came to talk to me. She was very locked into her problems, like this young man, suffering from a poor self-image, confused identity, failure in school, and a broken love affair. She, too, had concluded, "You're born, you live, you have children, you die; they have children, they die—it's an endless, senseless cycle. It's all a joke. Nothing makes sense."

Neither of these two young people had lived long enough to know that the problems they were feeling were universal, that each of us has to face one day the root question of who we are, why are we here, what this life—terminal, indeed—is all about.

There's a banner that was put up in churches in the 70s that held a strong clue to the answers. It said, "Unless you love somebody, nothing makes sense." I would profess the truth of that. But I've learned that it takes a quantum leap in our life before we can get from the womb to the point where we're actually capable of loving someone. Unfortunately, people like this young man and woman are stuck somewhere in mid-place.

Life does make sense, but not until we free ourselves from an immobility that prevents us from soaring out of the depths and into new life. How do we do this? It may sound outrageous, but in order to make sense of our lives and come to peace with our pain, each of us must surrender to a symbolic death. This isn't original. Jesus said it first, "Unless the seed dies, there can be no new life." He was giving us the blueprint for making sense out of our lives, and it wasn't an easy path. He said the starting point is the destruction of the encasement that keeps our potential and possibilities locked in the small container of self. The British-born poet W.H. Auden affirmed this in his line, "And life is the destiny you are bound to refuse until you have consented to die."

Once released from the prison of self, we can find purpose. Once we free ourselves from self-concentration, self-concerns, self-everything, we have the chance to soar and connect with the world—and with heaven as well. Or, put plainly, we can fly only after the cocoon has broken open.

That's the prize—the wings that bring the freedom to know the thrill of breathing forever, because it is Spirit, not air, that fills us, giving us a love-power that connects us with every other created being and with our Source, in joy and peace.

That's the Good News. But the bad news comes first, making it hard to keep our eyes on the prize. For this new life comes only after the destruction of the old, the one that's locked in the self, and the shattering can break us as well as make us. As for why it has to be this way, there is no answer that satisfies if we think only in terms of comfort and worldly ease. But if we accept that suffering has an important role when it comes to our relationship with God, then we can accept it and even come to see, strangely enough, the beauty in it.

Søren Kierkegaard, the 19th-century Danish philosopher, expressed this belief poetically in his "Christian Discourses."

> He who dreams must be awakened...and then comes affliction to awaken the dreamer, affliction which like a storm tears off the blossoms, affliction which nevertheless does not bereave of hope, but recruits hope....It does not bestow hope, but it recruits it. It is man himself who acquires it, this hope of eternity which is deposited in him, hidden in his inner man; but affliction recruits it.

Should one want an affirmation of Kierkegaard's reflection on the meaning of affliction, pick up Oscar Wilde's *De Profundis,* where he tells of his soul's journey:

> I bore up against everything with some stubbornness of will and much rebellion of nature till I had absolutely nothing left in the world but one thing. I had lost my name, my position, my happiness, my freedom, my wealth. I was a prisoner and a pauper. But I still had my children left. Suddenly they were taken away from me by the law. It was a blow so appalling that I did not know what to do, so I flung myself on my knees and bowed my head, and wept and said, "The body of a child is as the body of the Lord; I am not worthy of either." That moment seemed to save me. I saw then that the only thing for me was to accept everything. Since then—curious as it will no doubt sound—I have been happier. It was, of course, my soul in its ultimate essence that I had reached. In many ways, I had been its enemy, but I found it waiting for me as a friend.

Oscar Wilde had learned for himself the answer to the most important question, that is, as Ram Dass had expressed it to me, how to find peace from one's pain. He had to walk into his pain and let his heart break so that it would open wide enough to let God in. "The distance from our pain is our distance from God," says Stephen Levine, author of *Healing Into Life and Death*.

This is a truth the mystics knew well. The 13th-century German scholar-mystic Meister Eckhart used the analogy of skins to make this point:

> A man has many skins in himself, covering the depths of his heart...[and] soul....To get at the core of God at his greatest, one must first get into the core of himself at his least, for no one can know God who has not first known himself. Go to the depths of the soul, the secret place of the Most High, to the roots, to the heights; for all that God can do is focused there.

Christ, of course, said it first, "The Kingdom of God is within you." But the key to this kingdom is the sword of sorrow, and while peace and joy are found, once the mystery is accepted, the journey to the center of our being is a hazardous one.

Yet, over and over I find people who are living witnesses of this mystery—that by opening their heart to pain, they also opened it to love, and, so, found incredible peace. Because I have been a newspaper person, a writer of personality profiles, I was able to ask people questions that probed their depths. And I found inspiration and a soul-connection with so many.

I met Max Cleland when he was addressing a rehabilitation agency dedicated to helping people with disabilities gain independence. Max, who was head of the U.S. Veterans Administration under President Jimmy Carter and is currently secretary of state in Georgia, was perfectly qualified for the task. He himself is an inspiring example of someone who overcame great odds to make a life for himself. And he talks openly about the day that changed his life—Vietnam, April 8, 1968—when a grenade explosion left him a triple amputee, but "lucky to be alive."

"Not many people believed that a 25-year-old former Army captain, losing two legs and one arm, could do much after that," he told me. "Not many people saw many apples in that seed. But I was scared not to believe in myself and God."

Having the determination that he wanted his life to "mean something," gave him the courage not only to become healed, but to become "somebody." And he did, as his credentials show. "I don't look at myself as handicapped, but just severely inconvenienced," said the Atlanta-born gentleman, who told his story in a book he titled *Strong at the Broken Places,* taken from the Hemingway line: "Life breaks us all, and afterward many are strong at the broken places."

He spoke honestly of those years after his terrible wounds when he had to pull his life together, how he often became so discouraged that he would think that "doing the right thing is ending it all." He realized then that people who have extraordinary setbacks "have to dig down deeper...to discover more courage" than normally needed. And he learned a new definition of courage. "Before Vietnam I thought courage was the absence of fear." He learned, instead, that "courage is fear," courage means to "say our prayers and keep on moving....Courage is the ability to focus on opportunity in the face of danger, to take disabilities and turn them into possibilities...to turn your scars into stars."

Most important to his determination to live again was "the grace of God and the help of friends that gave me a lot of faith" to go ahead. Still, he said, with a handshake of enormous strength, "It is a battle I fight every day to keep the sense of myself and be the person God intended me to be."

Truly Max Cleland is a man whose great faith in God and life has been glowingly refined from the crucible of his pain.

Jeanne Mitchell Biancolli is a violinist in Connecticut, a very special person. After her debut in New York in 1947 she was called "a bright young star in the violin galaxy" and hit the big time. For a dozen years she pursued an impressive career, playing in numerous concert halls in the United States and around the world. She also made guest appearances on TV programs hosted by such then popular stars as Arthur Godfrey and Kate Smith.

Jeanne Mitchell gave up the world of performing when she married Louis Biancolli, music critic for the long defunct World Telegram and Sun. Motherhood followed, and after a few years, when her husband became unexpectedly ill, she turned to teaching to support her family.

A critical moment came in the early 70s when she lay near death with kidney failure and heart trouble. As the medical team worked on her, Jeanne, who had never thought much about God or prayer, found herself calling on God and telling herself, like a command, "This will not prevail. I will survive."

She did recover, and while she then tried to forget God, it didn't work. "We're all equipped with a window," she told me, "to see not only inside ourselves, but also to look out to see truth."

One day she found herself driving and suddenly crying, unable to stop the tears. She kept hearing the words inside her head, telling her "You haven't been good to God." She drove aimlessly and surprisingly came upon a sign that said "Abbey of Regina Laudis." She didn't even know what town she was in. She drove up to the place, not knowing what kind of a religious order she would find here. She was warmly welcomed by a nun, and later discovered that this was a monastery of Benedictines.

The sisters there "took me from nowhere to what I consider the end of the line—God," Jeanne Biancolli says today. She was baptized into the Catholic Church in March 1983. It was at that time that I met Jeanne, and concluded that her difficult life had been God's way of wooing her, in the spirit of Francis Thompson's poem, "The Hound of Heaven."

In putting her life in order and finding peace, Jeanne Biancolli, who lost her husband and one of her two daughters in the same year, said she came to realize that her music has always been a "spiritual quest." Now, she says, "I spend a lot of energy trying to play in tune." Her double meaning is obvious.

She calls living "a process like making bread. It has two or three risings. You beat it and it rises and beat it again and it rises again because the yeast, which takes its own direction, is working all the while. Now, in my

60s, I'm at the third rising," she says, using the analogy to describe her personal and spiritual growth. As for her music, it goes on beautifully. And when you hear her in concert, it's the sound of God's love that comes through this woman who has been beaten by life, but keeps on rising.

I interviewed actress Patricia Neal on the occasion of the publication of her autobiography *As I Am*. One of the first things she told me was, "I don't know why, but my life didn't go the way I intended. When I was young, I thought life would be a miracle, so sensational. I could hardly wait to live it. Then these horrendous tragedies happened," she said, waving a hand at her book, indicating the story was all there.

Her book tells of a life that unquestionably reads like a novel, one not overly kind to the heroine. It tells of a woman who loves but is rejected by a married man, who buries a child, who nearly loses another child in a freak accident, who is afflicted by a debilitating stroke, and who then faces the devastating rejection by her husband who leaves her for another woman.

The biggest sensation caused by the Patricia Neal story was the detailed account of her love affair with the late actor Gary Cooper, a relationship that led to a pregnancy and an abortion. Mr. Cooper waited in the car for her while the abortion was done and Ms. Neal wrote, "Afterward, we wept together." She said she regretted the decision ever since. "For 30 years, alone in the night, I cried. If I had only one thing to do over in my life, I would have that baby."

When I read the book, and as I spoke with Ms. Neal, what I found most remarkable was the role Maria Cooper, the actor's daughter, played in Ms. Neal's life. She was the one person to have been hurt the most from Ms. Neal's affair with her father. Yet, when the news media reported the actress' stroke, this lovely lady, Maria Cooper Janis, married to pianist Byron Janis, wrote to her.

"I cannot describe the feeling its generous greeting imparted, and I will never forget its three most important words: I forgive you," wrote Ms. Neal.

Later, Maria Cooper, who I am fortunate to be able to count among my friends, was to pop into Ms. Neal's life again, "like a miracle," and a sign that the grace of God was at work there. They bumped into each other in the lobby of a New York hotel. Sensing Ms. Neal's "inner anguish"—her husband had just left her—Ms. Cooper, a devout Catholic, spoke to her of God and of an Abbey in Bethlehem, Connecticut.

The actress, who still suffers from the effects of her stroke, found her way to this Abbey and it marked a major turning point in her life. The Lady Abbess counseled her to walk into her pain and write her story "insisting that I remember it all, so that I could begin to understand who I am and what I am called to do in this life." And Ms. Neal, who has remained close to the Abbey, said she came to see that the hand of God had been at work in her life, weaving a pattern that would finally bring her to peace.

As we came to the end of the interview, Ms. Neal's fine spirit came through again when she remarked,

"Life gets tough and sometimes it's hard to believe there's a light at the end of the tunnel. But you've got to have faith that it must be there. And sometimes, the only thing to do is smile."

CHAPTER SIX

LOOKING FOR MEANING

It was in the spring of '89 that I interviewed the great jazz artist Dave Brubeck. He was then 68 and had recently undergone triple bypass surgery. He told me neither he nor his wife Iola ever doubted that everything would go just fine. He explained why. "We had gone through so much already. By the time you reach this point in life, with this many kids, you know there's no way you're not going to have sorrow. But if you can't rise above it, you really don't have faith."

I could relate. In fact, when I began the interview, I told him we have two things in common—"six kids and the Catholic Church." I had read a few years back that the jazz musician had converted to Catholicism. I also knew from previous stories that he was a caring man. He once explained why. "Christ said it. Buddha said it, Martin Luther King said it: We must live together as brothers or die together as fools."

Perhaps because of his personal quest for meaning, Mr. Brubeck early on took a spiritual approach to his music and his life. He began writing religious oratorios and cantatas years ago, becoming an influential force in contemporary sacred music. He was commissioned to write special music for Pope John Paul II's visit to San Francisco in 1987.

Remarkably, one of his sacred pieces worked in reverse to radically influence the composer, leading to his baptism as a Roman Catholic in 1982. It came about, he said, after he "was doing something I had refused to do—write a Mass."

The chain of events began with a man named Ed Murray, involved with a religious center known as the Shrine of Our Lady of the Snows in Belleville, Illinois. "He would show up at concerts and he talked Mass until I did it." When the composer finished the Mass two years later, Ron Brassard, a priest he had met from Providence, Rhode Island, did the premier performance at St. Peter and Paul Cathedral in Philadelphia.

But—"Father Ron wanted to know why I had not written an Our Father in the Mass....Well, we were finished with the Mass as far as I could see and because of that, my wife, the kids and I went to the Caribbean for a vacation." One night while they were there something startling happened. "I dreamed the Our Father from beginning to end," he said, adding this convinced him he "ought to put it in the Mass."

The dream "started making me think more about the power of what was going on," said Mr. Brubeck. Subsequently, he followed his "call" and was baptized and confirmed at Our Lady of Fatima parish in Wilton,

Connecticut. Again I saw this as a story of a person who had faced sorrow, turned this into love, and was given a special grace by God, like a resounding "Amen!"

Marge Champion, another inspiring person, had her life shaken by tragedy, but was sustained by her spiritual moorings. Many will remember that she and her husband were the famed dancers, Marge and Gower Champion, who brightened so many shows with their choreography in the early days of television. Most would not know that she was the model for Snow White and other early Disney dancing characters, and also one of Shirley Temple's dancing teachers.

I interviewed Ms. Champion at her home in Massachusetts in 1992, and she was warm and open, telling me that in many ways she had a halcyon life for 60 years—career, success, two children, a divorce from Gower, but a friendly one, a remarriage, and then a new home in the hills of Massachusetts. But in 1980, life changed, beginning with the death of Gower, who died of a rare leukemia on the opening night of his hit show, *42nd Street*.

"Nine months later, my husband Boris was killed in a helicopter accident," Ms. Champion revealed, speaking of Russian director Boris Sagal, whom she married in 1976. "Then five years ago, my son Blake was killed in an accident on the road. He was 25, talented and gorgeous, with a zest for life."

She lost three people she loved, all in one decade. As for what sustained her during those traumas, it was certainly the support of friends, but also her strong faith. She expresses it simply. "There is a created order in the universe that no man could have dreamed of." And smiling, she asked, "Who put the stripes on the tiger?"

As I talked to this woman, still lovely and remarkably youthful at 72, it struck me that in a way she had been preparing for the blows that were to hit her. She had actually co-written two books, published by Word Books in Waco, Texas, that expressed her belief that people should worship the Lord—totally. These had come from a project begun in 1967 when she was an elder in the Bel Air California Presbyterian Church. One of her co-parishioners was an actress named Marilee Zdeneck and they formed a partnership "to develop more creative worship services...to involve more people so that everybody brought their talents to a service." It was time, she noted, using the expression of Pope John XXIII, to get some "fresh air" into worship.

Catch the Wind was their first book, a lively affirmation that worship should be total and free if one is to "feel" intimacy with God. The second was *God Is a Verb,* with photography assembled by Ms. Champion, who said that her experience as a dancer had led her to become aware that "the body is an instrument of praise to God." The title came from the late famed architect, Buckminster Fuller, whom they had met and who had impressed them with his words, "For God, to me, it seems, is a verb, not a noun."

A remarkably vibrant woman, Ms. Champion has grown more beautiful from her pain, still seeing the humor in life and ever striving to continue to "make a contribution" to the world. She spends much time caring for her trees and flowers, for her love of nature is also a conduit to God. All the growing beauty is "a blessing and a benediction," she says.

As I talked to this lovely woman, I remembered what priest-psychologist Father Adrian van Kaam said in a talk some years back, that as we get older, we should become "a blessed presence to others." I think Marge Champion fits that description. She has used her pain to further open her heart, and so, is filled with the joy of God.

One man I shall never forget, who ranks as one of the greatest people I have ever met, is Bill Genovese, a Vietnam veteran who lost both his legs in that war. Tragic as this was, it wasn't the first trauma he had to face and come to terms with. When he was 16, he had to cope with a devastating, senseless, criminal act—the murder of his sister Kitty Genovese.

Anyone who was around in the mid-60s remembers the tragic story of 28-year-old Catherine Genovese of Kew Gardens, Queens. She was stalked by a killer in the early morning hours of Friday, March 13, 1964, and for more than thirty minutes she was sexually assaulted and stabbed until her screams stopped and she was dead. Her story is remembered to this day because while she was being so brutally attacked, 39 so-called respectable citizens—her neighbors—heard her cry "please help me," but turned away. They did not want to get involved.

After his sister's death, Bill Genovese found himself struggling against anger. The issue that would not go away was "what do we owe each other? I was brought up to believe when your turn comes, you stand up. Part of the reason I went to Vietnam was to find myself. I was reacting to what I perceived was so much apathy," and he did not want to find apathy toward his country within himself, he said.

So at age 18 he went to Vietnam, and at 19 was in the wrong place when an explosive was detonated by "enemy natives. I didn't lose my legs there. But there was nerve damage and they became rotten infested...My legs were amputated later, horribly, bit by bit."

He was from the school of "gut it out," but life had dealt him two terrible blows before he was 19 and understandably he was feeling the need to find meaning in all this.

> I was one of the good ones, wasn't I? Why was all this happening to one family—my sister murdered, my mother who had a cerebral hemorrhage a year later that she fortunately survived, me with my legs gone, and my father dying of cancer at the age of 59.

The struggle that went on inside Bill Genovese took turns for the worst many times, but something within him kept pointing him in directions that made him believe that "darn it, I am going to win this struggle." He was open to the "good things" that life could still bring and meeting and marrying Dale, a nurse, was one. Their three children, their home, his job, his Catholic faith—all these he counts as more of the good. And, while he struggles with physical pain—especially the very real and overwhelming one called "phantom pain,"—and with anger that still can "flare up like a rocket," he never descends into bitterness.

"Life makes the sense you make out of it," Bill Genovese says, and he personally made the decision "not to sit on the sidelines of life....I want to play." He has learned the hard way that "life comes with no guarantees...and the unthinkable can happen." His struggle has put him on a spiritual path. He has been broken by life, but has put himself back together, energized by love, which he spreads by his very presence.

There are so many more stories I could tell, about people I have met who have walked head-on into their pain and grief, and when they had nothing left as props or disguises or masks, confronted their emptiness and loneliness, and to their surprise found that back at square one God was waiting for them.

They go and let "the seed die" so that they could have the promised "new life." They could have ostracized their pain, treated it with cold indifference, hardened themselves, shut God out, and let their lives turn into a hell. But they didn't. They knew, perhaps subconsciously, as Stephen Levine says, that "Deep within us...is a homesickness for God." If we will not enter into our pain, we will "never awaken the Beloved" within us and learn that "the path to joy is through our pain."

If we can find the courage to commit the symbolic

act of dying to ourselves, we become free, and, once free, once liberated from selfishness, we can get high on the realization that our origins are magnificent, for they come from the same one who—as God told Job—laid the cornerstone of the universe. Then we are capable of the most exquisite joy. Free of the self-package imprisoning the seed, we can blossom, bonded in love to others and to God. Then we can understand that we are not alone, but, as Cardinal Newman said, are "a link in a chain, a bond of connections between persons"; that we have a destiny—paradise; and that, because of all the above, we have a life that makes sense.

CHAPTER SEVEN

How Do We Begin
to Heal?

Three years ago, two of my grandchildren, then ages four and two, were in a very serious automobile accident. Their baby sitter was driving my daughter's car when it collided with a school bus, fortunately with no children on it. The babysitter Anamaria was close to death for several days, my four-year-old grandson Florian needed emergency surgery to save his life, and two-year-old Mikael came through bruised, but undamaged.

The accident and the next few weeks were understandably a nightmare for my daughter. On top of all the human suffering, there were the practical problems to deal with, like needing to find several thousands of dollars to get another car, and squabbling insurance companies dickering over the medical bills.

I was with my daughter one day about a month after the accident when she got an unpleasant call from the hospital wanting an immediate payment of $10,000. She fell apart. Life was unfair, she cried, full of pain and suffering. You never can get out from under, the world doesn't care about you. Why does God let things like this happen to the innocent? She complained the whole gamut, as we all have at times been tempted to do.

When she stopped to take a breath, I said, "Margee, you've spent enough time on the problems, now concentrate on solving them." She was infuriated with me, retaliating by saying, "Just because you can deal with pain and accidents and problems, just because you're strong, you think everybody else can be strong. Well, they can't."

I put my arms around her, and her husband, who is half French, half Vietnamese, looked at me and said tenderly, "She has reached her limits."

He was being patient and philosophical, but I said what I had to say. "Well, kids, when you reach your limits, there's only one place to go—beyond your limits."

It sounded momentarily harsh, but it was the truth. The world had broken her and she was at the point where she would either stay broken or begin the healing process that would make her strong. She had to know that to begin the healing, you have to go beyond your limits.

I have known so many who have been broken by life. I met them because of my own experience of divorce and a book I wrote about single parenting. I was asked often to give talks to Catholics around the country who were in a situation similar to my own, either because of divorce or widowhood. And my knowledge that separation, divorce, and death are weapons of destruction was reaffirmed over and over again. Our mission then was to repair the damage by going beyond any limits we had accepted before—to rebuild, get strong again, and maybe come out better than we were.

Not one of us had a magic pill to make this happen. We each had to find our way in going beyond our limits—hampered by all the things that were there to block us.

I think for all of us there was first the sense of being cheated. We had begun our young adult years with great expectations. Certainly we had entered our marriages believing we would live happily ever after—for life. But our great expectations were shattered and we had to learn, as Margaret Mitchell expresses well in *Gone With the Wind*, "Life is under no obligation to give us what we expect."

Then we all had to deal with a changed self-image and cope with it. This certainly involves not only how we view ourselves but also how others—like family, neighbors, church, etc., view us. Certainly in my day—back in the 60s—the terms divorced woman and working mother had terrible connotations. Those terms depicted two great menaces to society. We were put in a box labeled "defective person," "neglecter of children," "easy mark for guys on the prowl."

For Catholics, this certainly was the image of failure. Marriage and family sermons had always been based on the model of the Holy Family and projected the theory that perfect sacrifice in marriage makes all problems bearable. I met more than one priest who sloughed off my very serious marriage problems by telling me, as I have already mentioned, to find the courage to carry my cross. I did, too, for 18 years, until I saw that my cross had been cloned six times over with my kids each carrying one they had never contracted for!

Also blocking the healing, for myself and most of the other single parents I met, were real practical problems that brought on real fear. And all this was happening at a time when our lives had been radically altered because of the divorce or death and our self-image clobbered. Understandably, under circumstances like these, we get somewhat immobilized because moving into the unknown is fraught with uncertainties and ambiguities. After the trauma of an ended marriage, we feel like we're drowning in deep water, unable to swim, watching our water wings float away.

Yet, we really are in a sink-or-swim situation, like being aboard an Italian airline that was in big trouble. To assure the passengers, the pilot said, "We're experiencing some difficulty and are asking all passengers who can swim to go to the right side of the plane. All who can't swim, go to the left. Now in a few minutes when we hit the water, those of you on the right start swimming and in about a mile you'll reach land. Those on the left—thank you for flying Alitalia!"

Well, on the "drowning" side, just consider as one example the financial disaster that hits so many newly disrupted families, even when the non-custodial parent responsibly makes support payments. I was making $125 a week in 1968 when I was left with six kids. I was supposed to get $60 a week from their father but that came in only sporadically at first and then not at all. I moonlighted, wrote articles till two in the morning, getting physically exhausted. I worried constantly about whether I was properly supervising my children. I could write a book about the distress calls I got in those years, kids always needing me—like Peter, age six, falling out of a tree; pipes in the house in the winter time freezing and bursting; Paul stranded on the road with a broken-down car; Margee playing hooky; John in a motorcycle accident. I know most single parents can match my stories.

In those days, washing machine going, kids climbing the walls, phone ringing, I often felt like the mother who collapsed in a chair and moaned out loud "If only I had loved and lost!"

Certainly another pitfall I found to be common among the single parents I met, one that blocked our excursion into healing and strength after the wounds of death and divorce, is what I came to recognize as fear of maturity. This is a problem that affects all too many people suffering losses and other blows. We don't want to face the fact that the time has come for us to take full responsibility for our lives, and so we fall back on easy excuses.

The excuses I've heard could fill a humor book. You want to take a course, but you're afraid you can't do the work. You want to go to a concert but you're too lethargic to go out at night. You want to lose weight, but you can't give up ice cream because it relaxes you.

Excuses stop us dead and make it impossible for healing to begin. It's the "yes, but" syndrome. Excuse-making is such a prevalent condition it now has the fancy name "defensive avoiding."

If we examine our excuses with real honesty, we know that most of them don't make sense. They sound classically like the one I call the master of excuses. It was made by the lover from the 60s Italian movie "Seduced and Abandoned." First the guy gets the young girl pregnant, and then he's got this terrible problem. He can't marry her, he wails, "because she's not a virgin."

We never heal if we get too enamored of defensive avoiding. Anyone who falls into the trap of constantly finding excuses for inaction should hang this great piece of wisdom on their wall; "Remember, you can fly, but first the cocoon has to go."

The unexpected blows brought by life can indeed be traumatic and make us feel angry, depressed, abandoned, our lives out of control.

Some fall into self-pity, the worst possible condition of all. I remember giving a talk in the early 70s when I had helped to start the first program for Divorced and Separated Catholics in the Rockville Centre diocese on Long Island. I was giving an upbeat talk about how we didn't have to accept labels like "broken family," that all of us have it in our power to rebuild our lives and our families, and to be on guard over the traps we have faced, one of them being self-pity. We can stay so busy feeling sorry for ourselves that we can miss life's parade, I said.

One woman got up and literally screamed at me that she had a right to feel sorry for herself because her husband had left her for a younger woman after twenty years of marriage. I told her that if she wanted to sit in a corner and suck her thumb, that was her business, and if she wanted to justify her giving up on life by calling it her *right*, that was her business, too. Only she ought to know the price she'd pay for this. She'd stay wounded and never get on with the healing that could make her strong, make her a person again. I wonder what ever happened to her?

Other traps that block healing are drugs, and I'm not talking cocaine. I'm talking tranquilizers and sleeping pills. I remember a woman I worked with who had gone through an unpleasant divorce. She opened her purse one day, and I swear she was a walking pharmacy. I read a statistic a few years ago that 14 million prescriptions for tranquilizers were written in one year in New York State. That's a lot of sedation, and you can't get strong while you're sedated. Another very popular drug is still alcohol. In abusive quantities this is another block to any kind of healing.

What accounts for why some people heal and grow strong and others don't? I think that healing begins with faith, a conviction that we have choices and that these choices begin with an attitude that somehow makes us believe "every kick is a boost."

I'm not talking about a Mickey Mouse kind of faith.

I'm talking about strong faith. I'll give an example. My sister Loretta, a physical therapist who works with AIDS patients and disabled senior citizens, mostly black women on welfare, tells me she's learned about faith from her patients. One woman told her: "Honey, faith means that when you pray for rain, you bring an umbrella."

Armed with this kind of faith, convinced there's a God who loves us and listens to us, healing can begin, because we have the tools needed to begin believing again in our own power. That's not easy in a world that often seems determined to knock us down again.

In 1968, all I had was $5,000 after my divorce. My Italian father had always talked to me of the importance of having your own home when you had children and I wanted a home. In those days you could still buy one for under $20,000. I started looking and found one that was perfect—for $16,000. When I got back to the office with the real estate agent, he asked me where my husband worked. "I have no husband," I told him, "I'm buying the house." He looked at me infuriated. "Why are you wasting my time?" he yelled. "You can't buy a house. You'd never get a bank to give you a mortgage."

I went home and I was angry. Those words, "you can't" stung me. I had been hearing them over and over since becoming a single parent: You can't do a good job being a parent alone: You can't work day and night: You can't make enough money to educate them: You can't get a credit card. You can't, you can't, you can't.

They were all telling me I was powerless. I thought of the Latin root for power, potency—to be able. I realized people were constantly trying to take my power away from me and I resolved then and there that the *instant* anyone said to me, "you can't" I would be on guard. I would know the game and I wouldn't play.

The next day I called a priest friend. "I need a man," I told him. We went together to the real estate office. The two men talked about "her" as if I weren't there. It was finally decided that "she" could probably take over the existing mortgage on the house, because my $5,000 bridged the distance between the mortgage and the selling price.

But what I learned was priceless. I learned that if I believed in my own power and found a way to exercise it, I could keep my power. Actually, I could strenghten it—something all of us must do to be healed.

I grant you, to see troubles this way requires great optimism. Long ago I read that the Chinese word for crisis is divided into two characters. One means danger, but the other means opportunity. Whoever developed that Chinese written word manifested tremendous savvy. He—or maybe she?—understood that we should have the honesty to recognize the dangers involved in the existing crisis or situation, but should also have the wisdom to recognize that the crisis opens opportunities for us to change our lives for the better.

I caution you, however, not to overdo this optimism bit. My kids have had to live with someone who was always saying things like "When life gives you lemons, make lemonade." Or "Worry is the interest you pay on money you never borrowed." I agree, it was a bit much.

My favorite optimism story was the answer of St. Francis de Sales to a man complaining that roses have thorns. The eminent saint responded, "Nay, rather isn't it wonderful that thorns have roses." Which inspired my son John one day, who was not in a mood for one of my gems, to respond—with appropriate gesture and a big grin—"Watch out, Mom, thorns have roses but faces have noses!"

Which brings me to the next point about gaining strength after being broken. It'll never happen without a sense of humor. Laughter is still the greatest medicine, and this means, of course, not taking ourselves too seriously.

If any of you need encouragement, you should get in touch with the Fellowship of Merry Christians, based in Kalamazoo, Michigan. I just love that name, and the name of their publication, The Joyful Noise letter. You find wonderful tidbits in there, like how St. Teresa of Avila would pray, "From somber, serious, sullen saints, save us, O Lord!"

Another condition for healing is an obvious one— good motivational patterns. It helps if all your life you've been a person who knows that wishing won't make it so. For to heal and grow strong requires action, undertaken from a firm, internal base. What does this mean? Several things. You have to be a person convinced of your own self-worth. You have to be able to understand your part so as not to fall into repeat, negative situations. This brings to mind the oft-quoted line: "Those who don't remember history are bound to repeat its mistakes."

You have to be able to clarify a direction for yourself so that you have a road map for where you want to go. You have to be able to analyze your own behavior patterns, that is, have insights about what makes you tick.

Most importantly you have to believe that it is up to you to create your own personal definition of success. No one can supply the definition that applies to you. And finally, you have to be able to recognize your personal achievements, regardless of what others think or say.

All of this takes courage, and I think courage is what is needed most of all if we are to grow strong at the broken places. We tend to be afraid of the word courage, possibly because we think of it in epic proportions—related to life and death issues: war, heroic rescues, crime fighting, and public honesty in the political arena. We seem unwilling to call smaller acts of heroism courage.

There are several quotes about courage that clarify what this word means. One is from Ludwig Borne: "True courage is not only a balloon for rising but also a parachute for falling."

Another comment about courage is attributed to a woman named Victoria Lincoln who said: "This is the art of courage: to see things as they are and still believe that the victory lies not with those who avoid the bad, but those who taste in living awareness every drop of the good."

It may sound simple, but to live with courage is not easy. In fact, I saw one day on the wall of a senior center in Connecticut a test that lets us get down to the bone to see how each of us rates. It said:

There are first of all *Wishbones*—those who wish somebody would do something about their problem. There are *Jawbones*—those who talk but do nothing else. There are *Knucklebones*—those who knock everything. And then there are *Backbones*—those who carry the load and do the work. Which are you?

CHAPTER EIGHT

GOD GETS CLOSER
—BLOW BY BLOW

Sometimes family members talk about their own mortality and death and the perspective is merely philosophical. When my brother Joe and I talk about that subject, it is deeply personal. My brother, eight years younger than I, has lived with a time bomb in his body for 20 years. He has a malignant condition called "hairy cell leukemia."

I well remember a late afternoon in 1973 when I had a sudden urge to get in touch with my seven brothers and sisters, who all still lived in or near our hometown of Albany, New York, about 250 miles from where I then lived on Long Island. It was about four in the afternoon, but I urgently wanted to call, so, I ignored the fact that they would wonder why I was calling long distance at this hour. I dialed my older sister, Rosemary.

She first commented on my "vibes" and then gave me the news that Joe, then 37, had just come out of hours of surgery, having had his spleen—enlarged to nearly 30 inches—removed. The news was bad. The prognosis was that he had an inoperable malignancy. Without medication, Joe would live six months, with medication, maybe two years.

We're a close famiy, unusually blessed with good health. The fact that one of us had become vulnerable to an illness was not only shocking, but unacceptable. We bombarded the Lord with prayers. Joe recovered temporarily, enough to be called a medical marvel, able to work and care for his family in spite of his condition.

But then, about seven years after my brother had been stricken with leukemia, just as he began to feel life could be sweet again, his wife, Jodi, then in her mid-thirties, was also devastatingly stricken with cancer. She had to undergo radical surgery for the removal of a breast and lymph nodes. She needed chemotherapy for a year, treatments that left her physically ill.

In the years that followed, my brother and sister-in-law had to undergo repeated hospitalizations and treatment. They joked that when they got into their car, it went on automatic pilot straight to St. Peter's Hospital! In 1986, we spent a lot of time in that place. Joe's condition was badly deteriorating. His doctor told us he had "nothing left for Joe." And, then, miraculously, a drug called interferon was approved, found effective for one form of cancer, hairy cell leukemia! Again, our prayers had been answered. Joe responded well to the interferon, going into remission.

Yet, for all these repeated blows, rarely did Joe and Jodi show self pity or complain. Their only wish was to live long enough to see their two young children, Joe, Jr. and Julie, get old enough to be able to make it on their own.

They remained hospitable to their family and friends and kept a sharp sense of humor. Joe used to quip that he was like Tevye in "Fiddler on the Roof," a little tired of being one of the "chosen people," wondering, like Tevye, couldn't God once in a while "choose somebody else!"

Then, as the new year of 1990 rang in, the worst blow of all hit Joe, when his beloved Jodi died, at age 48. He reproached the Lord, asking, "Why her, Lord, why not me? I was sick first. I should have been the one to go." He became angry at God, tried to turn away, looked inside himself and saw only bitterness. And then he surrendered, accepting that, as C.S. Lewis said, "Earth is not our permanent home." As his faith began to return, he found that the music he and Jodi loved would suddenly play on the radio at unexpected times, and he could feel her blessing. She came to him, too, in a dream, where she was at a banquet, radiant and happy. He accepted the messages and embraced the lesson.

If ever a faith was tested, my brother's was. Such testing happens to people who seem to get unjustly bombarded with recurring incidences of pain. They understandably grow tired from years and years of uncertainty and sorrow. Even for the family members, who stay by the side of suffering loved ones, faith is strained. We saw what Joe and Jodi went through, with their bodies cut into, bombarded with foreign substances called medicine, burned through with radiation that leaves red scorch marks on the skin, kept alive with transfusions of other people's blood. Yes, faith gets wobbly, and God's ways seem bitter, indeed.

Yet, as these blows came closer and grew stronger, they put Joe in a different place, the hidden space deep inside where "soul searching" takes over. It was a powerful new journey in a search for God, one that spilled over to me, covering me with a gift I call inspiration.

I had heard Joe often talk of death, but never of fear. When you have to face your own mortality as vividly and for as long as he has, death is no longer a stranger. It becomes almost personified, like a companion. After you go through the shock and anger of discovering the presence of death in your body, you can reach a stage where you, strangely enough, find a new peace. You see the world's power plays for advancement, success, and money as a senseless charade. "I wanted to be a millionaire when I was 20," Joe told me once, with a laugh that showed the disdain he had come to feel for such empty values.

Because of Joe's illness, we who loved him also came to understand how, when we are well, we get caught up in the "comfort mode," locked into *things,* albeit important, like a job, money, a house, our appearance, and so on.

But when we face the truth that life is tentative, we get to the naked core of what is ultimately important.

In a word, love. When life is shaky, all you want is to touch the ones you love. Nothing else matters. For now you know that nothing else is lasting but love. And now you want the love that is everlasting. In a word, God.

My brother's illness, Jodi's death, and the other traumatic blows life has hit my family with showed me this truth and made me wonder why we crowd out love so often, filling our lives with things that—when life becomes tentative—look only like junk. I have become convinced that it takes the blows to get the blinders off so that we can see, really see, what is important and get wise enough to ask: Why have I been given this life, and what is it that I am supposed to do in the time I have been given?

One of the most touching affirmations of this came from the heart of a critically acclaimed writer of short fiction, Andre Dubus. This New Englander was struck by a car and permanently disabled in 1986. His book *Broken Vessels* is a collection of essays he wrote between 1977 and 1990, and contains these lines:

> After the dead are buried, and the maimed have left the hospitals and started their new lives, after the physical pain of grief has become, with time, a permanent wound in the soul, a sorrow that will last as long as the body does, after the horrors become nightmares and sudden daylight memories, then comes the transcendent and common bond of human suffering, and with that comes forgiveness, and with forgiveness comes love.

God does, indeed, get closer, blow by blow.

Commenting in a *New York Times* essay on how this passage shows "the spiritual maturation that suffering can force," writer Nancy Mair wrote: "The life that leads one to this point can no longer be termed in any sense disastrous."

I've kept another newspaper clip that gave an affirmation of how God blasts into our hearts. This was a segment written by the late Lee Atwater, the political campaigner for George Bush who became infamous for his tactics, especially in engineering the 1988 Willie Horton incident to discredit the Democratic candidate Michael Dukakis as being soft on criminals.

When Mr. Atwater was dying of brain cancer in 1991, he converted to Catholicism and made a plea for forgiveness, as reported in *Life* magazine:

My illness helped me to see that what was missing in society is what was missing in me: a little heart, a little brotherhood. The 80s were about acquiring—acquiring wealth, power, prestige. I know I acquired more wealth, power, and prestige than most. But you can acquire all you want and still feel empty....

It took a deadly illness to put me eye-to-eye with that truth, but it is a truth that the country, caught up in its ruthless ambitions and moral decay, can learn on my dime. I don't know who will lead us through the 90s, but they must be made to speak to this spiritual vacuum at the heart of American society, this tumor of the soul.

Certainly another man who experienced a spiritual change as a result of an unexpected and devastating trauma is Moorehead Kennedy, Jr., one of the U.S. hostages in Iran during the Carter presidency. I remember reading a headline in *The New York Times* during Lent of 1981 that said, "Ex-Hostage and Wife Speak of Spiritual Change." The story told of how Mr. Kennedy and his wife Louisa maintained that the 444 days of captivity in Iran had led each to a "deeper spiritual transformation."

Addressing a congregation at the Episcopal Cathedral of St. John the Divine in Manhattan that Lent, Mrs. Kennedy likened the early stages of the ordeal to a "crucible of anguish" which later turned into a "golden bowl" containing the "experience of God and how one reaches out to God and finds there everything one needs."

I read that and was, again, inspired. I felt it is fortunate that few of us are or will ever be hostages in such a dramatic way. Nevertheless, we all have hostage moments—times when we are trapped, stuck in an uncomfortable or painful situation. These can be, as Mrs. Kennedy said, "a crucible," a time for burning out the residues of this world, all the false values and distorted desires of the ego that envelop us. They can be the occasion as well for burning away whatever immobilizes us, whatever keeps us from moving along in the faith journey that leads to God and to life forever.

On the other hand, we can stay hostages all our lives, responding to the blows by asking "why," which really means "why me?" Two years ago, I interviewed

Diane Berger, a mother who was suddenly hit with the trauma of seeing her 18-year-old son swept into the malestroms of manic depression. She had to face the terrible truth that her son had changed virtually overnight from a friendly, bright, athletic, talkative teenager to a gaunt stranger, tormented by voices, given to violent behavior and spewing nonsensical monologues. She had a good answer to "Why me?"

"We tend to ask, why me?" she told me, "but my father always said that if we ask that of the bad things, we have to ask it of the good, too."

She tried to pull together the pieces of their shattered lives by learning facts about her son's illness, but everything she could find was written in hard-to-understand, impersonal tones. So she wrote the book she herself had needed and it was published by William Morrow, titled *We Heard the Angels of Madness: One Family's Struggle With Manic Depression.*

As for pain, oh yes, it permeates her life. "We manage to chop it up and distribute it in the corners of our self, because if we lift it in one hunk, we wouldn't be able to get ourselves out the door," she said, with expressive imagery. She is "in a healing process," and reveals, "I don't hassle the small stuff any more." This degree of trauma and pain "gives you a very clear focus on what's important in life. It's a process that makes you much more sensitive to the world around you, and you do become more forgiving of the world," she said.

Yet, not everyone would grow as Diane Berger is

doing. Some would still ask "Why me?" and would never heal. For the more one stays in a screaming mode, feeling abused and victimized, the more one stays trapped in the sterile, resisting shell. The seed, with the new life within it, is put on hold, and one never learns the lessons that should come with the "dark night," to use the expression coined by St. John of the Cross:

"The 'otherness' of God impresses itself upon the person in the dark night. The soul is softened, loses arrogance, and grows in reverence. Life's journey is on sacred ground and we learn to show respect and remove our sandals," writes Carmelite Father John Welch in his beautiful essay "Introduction to John of the Cross," in the Paulist Press book, *When Gods Die*. How sad it is when a person becomes hardened by the blows of life and never comes to recognize that "life's journey is on sacred ground." I remember a young man, a good Christian, telling me of the pain he and his wife were going through. His mother-in-law had died, and without consulting her children, had willed her body to a medical school, requesting the school to cremate her remains when it had finished with them. Her children, grown and in their 30s, were crushed.

The mother had been a sour woman, difficult to get along with, a person who sowed discord, an alcoholic, prone to use guilt to manipulate her children—for surely they would have to feel guilty if they did not approve her willing her body for research that could possibly benefit someone else.

Yet, her son-in-law believed the woman had managed to inflict pain on her children even in death. She did this by denying them any knowledge of her plans and also by denying them a time to grieve their mother's death at a dignified burial. And then he added the saddest epitaph, in a tone that held only distress: "That woman made me a worse person by coming into my life."

I shuddered in reaction to his comment and all it said about someone who should have made him a better person because she had borne the woman he loved. I reacted with revulsion at the son-in-law's comment because he had described a relationship between family members that was terrible, and now it was too late to change it. The mother-in-law would have no second chance to mellow, or soften, or learn what she was supposed to have learned from life. She had lived her years and left her mark. The pain of her life had altered her, not for the better, but for worse.

I often think of a quote that has been attributed to Michaelangelo: "I do not carve a statue out of marble; I release the form that is within." I have sometimes used that imagery, believing that while we enter this world like unshaped marble, there is a final form that each of us is supposed to achieve. It doesn't happen by wishing, but by pounding and polishing. The end result is an incarnation, for we have then achieved our final form—the spiritual identity—that really was our destiny from all eternity.

CHAPTER NINE

WE ARE NEVER ALONE

The wonderful thing is that we are never alone in our pain. We have so many models to study, to pray to, to emulate. One of mine was the Jesuit priest-poet Gerard Manley Hopkins.

I first became acquainted with Hopkins in 1966 when I was at one of the lowest points in my life. My marriage was disintegrating; I was working day and night to care for and provide financial support for my children; I was feeling the effects of this relentless strain physically and the future looked desolate.

A priest I went to for counseling put a book in my hands. When I went home I read for the first time some of the most astounding poetry. The lines grabbed my attention and I could relate to them.

I cast for comfort I can no more get
by groping round my comfortless, than blind
eyes in their dark can day, or thirst can find
thirst's all in all in a world of wet.

And there were other lines, like, "I wake and feel the fell of dark, not day," and the astounding lines:

> When, when, peace, will you peace? I'll not play hypocrite to my own heart. I yield you do come sometimes; but that piecemeal peace is poor peace. What pure peace allows alarms of war, the daunting wars, the death of it?

I had found someone who knew, someone who understood, someone who had gone through despair, someone who could cry out to God his feelings of abandoment. Hopkins became my "mentor," the voice, or better yet, the brother who gave me permission to say with him, "Hope had grown gray hairs. Hope had mourning on."

Naturally I wanted to learn more about this man I found myself relating to so surely. He was the first of eight children (I am the second of eight children); his educated parents were fairly prosperous and devout Anglicans. Young Gerard went to Oxford University and was influenced by the Roman Catholic convert and future cardinal, John Henry Newman, who received him into the Roman Catholic Church. Hopkins entered the Jesuits, worked both as a teacher and parish priest, wrote fewer than 50 poems, virtually none published in his lifetime, accepted the pain of that blockage of his creativity, and died on June 8, 1889, at age 44.

Fortunately for the world, Robert Bridges, named Britain's poet laureate in 1913, was Hopkins's classmate and friend at Oxford. Bridges saved the poetry Hopkins sent him and in 1918, nearly 30 years after Hopkins's death, had it published.

What characterized Hopkins in his work and his life was his absolute awe of individuality and independence of spirit. Because so much in life blocks both the recognition and practice of these values, his frustration had to be enormous.

Hopkins always felt as if he had accomplished nothing of much importance. The fact that he suffered a great deal from poor health did not help either. No wonder he saw himself as "time's eunuch" and endured the agonies of near despair so powerfully expressed in his later poems.

Yet the verses that gave me so much strength are not the voice of despair. They are the cry for God's hand, with Hopkins's hand raised high in waiting. Only one who has deep and true faith can utter that cry. Hopkins did and had the courage to share that cry with others. His dying words were, "I am so happy, I am so happy." I wanted to understand how someone who had been pummeled so severely by external and internal pains could reach that point of happiness. And one day it became clear that it was the pummeling that had cleared away the debris causing his pain. And so, the man who had been given such extraordinary eyes to see that "The world is *charged* with the grandeur of God" could soar home joyfully.

Back in the 60s when I was first reading Hopkins, I was at a very traumatic time in my life. I felt much like the Oxford scholar, Chad Walsh, who had written a book called *Behold the Glory*. In it he admitted:

> It is extraordinarily difficult to love God whole-
> heartedly; to love one's neighbor, even when he
> is lovable, is no easier. I know what I should do;
> there is nothing in the teachings of Christ that is
> clearer: go and love. But knowledge is one thing,
> deed another. It seems as though I am two per-
> sons. One agrees with Christ and issues the ap-
> propriate orders. The other, with his own
> peculiar serenity, plays deaf, and continues to
> live as though my ego were the central point of
> the cosmos and all galaxies revolved around it.

I could relate. Here I was, a Catholic woman in the
60s, with a big family, my life in disarray, feeling abandoned by God and man, vulnerable to desolation and
despair. When I was divorced in 1967, I was left with
the total job of raising the children, and being almost
their sole financial support, an incredibly difficult position to be in. When you are so immersed in problems,
incessant work, daily confrontation with prejudices,
and other assorted pains, you come dangerously close
to asking, with Jesus, "My God, My God, why have
you forsaken me?" The spiritual turmoil gets expressed
in other questions, too. You wonder, if God is a loving
God, why has my life become so difficult, so bleak, so
lonely?

I was on a collision course with the "moment of
truth" about my relationship with God. This is almost
universally experienced by people who undergo a cri-

sis of such intensity that it threatens their very existence. It can be divorce, the death of a loved one, an attack upon the physical body by illness, accident or war, depression, alcoholism, being the victim of a crime, being parents of a child who commits suicide or flaunts the law or dies from an accident or illness, and even the shock of confronting one's own limitations, and, perhaps, sins. Traumas such as these can shake us to our very roots so that we are forced to look at the rock bottom questions: What is this existence all about anyway? Who needs it? Who wants it?

At this level, people trained in a religious tradition usually experience the shock of learning rather suddenly that old cliches don't work any more. When you are in a new, threatening place, you need a new scenario about what's happening between you and God; otherwise, religion and spirituality make no sense. That's where I was in the late 60s.

I remember I had read a story, I believe in the *New Yorker,* written by Mary McCarthy. It was about a girl in a convent school who, on a lark to get attention, had decided to tell the sisters and the priest-chaplain that she had "lost her faith." Before the static was over, a strange thing happened to her. She had, indeed, lost her faith. The story ended with her leaving the school, feeling as she had years earlier when she was just learning to swim, discovering way out in the deep water that her water wings were floating way behind her.

That's how I felt then. I was inexperienced, in water over my head, and I had lost my water wings, the security of my childish faith. Regardless of what the traumas are that alter lives, if we truly want to make sense of life, we have to get over the fear of drowning. We have to recognize that we are at a new starting point in the massive task of self-restoration and growth. This gives us hope.

For me, personally, being divorced and a single parent compelled me to examine my own personality, my values, my faith, and the meaning of spirituality from the perspective of unfamiliar external and internal environments. Each agony brought me closer to recognizing that my divorce, which was a severance from a human relationship, was parallel to the pain of being disconnected from God. Divorce made me yearn for the miracle of reconnection, the gift of being able to pick up the pieces of a shattered life and build a new, radically different one.

Each struggle led me to a place where I had not been before. I think I could call this "progress" in my quest for a spiritual maturity. I was discovering little by little, pain by pain, what it was that God wanted me to learn. At this time, I was reminded of an analogy given by Father Hans Küng at a five-day theology conference in Montreal in 1966. He was speaking on the need for re-interpretation of Scripture, explaining that this did not imply that anything new was being added to the original message. It was more that the original message was still being discovered.

Küng likened this to walking into a dark room and turning on a lamp. The area around the lamp would be disclosed and you could believe that you had now seen everything in that room. But suppose another light went on, disclosing yet some other furnishings. Your knowledge and vision would then be greatly broadened because you now had more information about the room.

People who are pummeled by pain are in a position where the darkened corners of themselves come to light with many surprises. One thing you find is that you have little patience with pat answers that are supposed to say something profound about the difficulties of your life. We become too often the recipients of a pop-religiosity. People don't know how to react to you and your troubles, so they tend to cover their ignorance by giving you nice and easy God-talk. "Put everything into God's hands...Just do what Jesus would do...God sends suffering to those he loves most...The back was made for the burden...Carry your cross and you'll get your reward in heaven." All this genre of advice is a turnoff. It is fuzzy. It trivializes spirituality.

My sister Rosemary had spent the last twenty years watching her husband deteriorate from Parkinson's disease and, later, colon cancer, until he died in March 1993. About ten years ago, she was very depressed. Her condition was compounded by the fact that she is a deeply religious Catholic and always believed that if she loved God enough, she would be accepting her problems better, would not be depressed, and would find peace.

She had gone to a priest for help. He told her she does too much talking when she prays and that if she would stop talking to God and start listening, she would hear a message from God. It didn't happen.

She went to another priest who said, "Your problem is that you have never had a love affair with Jesus." She asked me how to do that and I told her I thought it might be difficult to arrange. A nun told her to "let go and let God," but didn't provide a blueprint for showing her how.

I told my sister that in my opinion, any similarity between real religion and this God-language was less than coincidental. She had been asking for help and she was given slogans, tailored like a Madison Avenue hard-sell—quick, catchy, frothy. I suggested that such God-language works better for people who are "saved," sure of their spirituality, sure of their terms.

But for the majority of us pilgrims, our journey to God is on rougher territory. God gave us life and we will eventually return to God. We're not arguing that. But in between, *we* put on the coffee, make the bread, give birth to the children, deal with our conflicts, bury our dead, and struggle for peace. Pummeled people need words with substance, assurance with clout that we can cement the pieces of our lives together, and without bitterness towards God or others, struggle to regain wholeness once more. Rather than "carry your cross," wouldn't it be better to hear, "love your life because it came from God," and trust that with origins like this, you're made of the right stuff for getting through the pain?

I must admit that the God I was introduced to in my past rigid religious training was not a God I related to when my life was in disarray. The lonely, suffering Jesus came to my rescue in daily living, becoming my role model for faith. As my life was being battered, I was being drawn, perhaps by Jesus, to go for the heavy duty faith. I felt a yearning to be a part of all the grandeur, the motion, the unknowns of the universe. I wanted to understand my existence in terms of eternity. I wanted *God*.

It was in reading Teilhard de Chardin that I came close to finding what I was searching for. The vision of this remarkable French priest-scientist was on the wide screen of the universe, embracing the eternal. It crashed through the borders of history, science, and earthly life itself, and encircled the real glory—the universe recreated by the fires of love and merged with God.

Teilhard believed that what humans really had to be engaged in was the building of what he called one "immense organism," whose destiny is a "universal convergence" in God. The psychic energy for this work, he said, is love. "Picture an earth," he wrote, "where all men are clearly and primarily decided on advancing together to a passionately desired Being."

That would be a world without war, hate, destructive power, and all negative human restrictions. I might add, a world without divorce and destructive human relationships. Teilhard's world would be an earth transformed because the evolution that is really needed by humankind—spiritual evolution—would then be complete.

That was a vision I could buy. It led me to find the God I was seeking, the one I could trust was full of love, even when I didn't understand his ways. It was a mind blower to me to realize that God is the Source of Life, so full of love, that at one point, this Source literally burst, out of love, spilling life everywhere—like sparks from some gigantic, benevolent explosion. The sun, the stars, the earth, the animals, you and I are those sparks. We are made out of life and love.

No matter how down I get, with my pains, sufferings, and loneliness, in my setbacks to be a good person and a good parent, this realization pulls me back up. Whenever I remember my origins—that I am connected to the Source of Life itself, created out of love, nothing keeps me down. I get restored in joy and understand the truth of the saying that "joy is the sign of God in us."

I have no formulas for how to get one's conflicts under control, achieving peace and finding happiness. But I have learned that if we can accept the pain, the suffering, the loneliness, the pummeling of our hearts, as God's way of asking us to grow toward him, we can find meaning in life. If we can accept life with its sufferings as a way to a fuller realization of our capacity to be bonded to others, to nature, and to the very Source of Life, we can expand our circle of loved ones and stay conscious always of the wonder of living.

If we can get through the seemingly relentless fog, learning that, depending on our response, the blows are only a vehicle for us to make straight a path for the Lord, we can find the light again that brings back the sweetness of life.

CHAPTER TEN

TURNING DRAGONS INTO PRINCESSES

I grew up in an environment of women, Italian women, talkative, loud, loving, and emotional, who generally were either complaining or rejoicing, putting the blame or the credit, like second nature, squarely on God. It was either a tirade about how awful life was because there wasn't enough money, or because they were full of aches and pains, their husbands were inconsiderate and their children were selfish. Or, it was an aria about how much God loved them because some prayer had been answered.

I can still hear my grandmother saying *gratia* to the Lord, translated "thanks." I remember as a teenager reflecting one day on how interesting it was that in Italian, the word for thanks is "gratia," which could also be translated "grace."

Grace, of course, was a word I grew up hearing in Catholic school. We prayed for God's grace, calling it a gift, and we repeated St. Paul's saying: "There go I but for the grace of God." Only when I was older did I catch the real meaning of this word, that grace described a link between us and God; that grace was God's free, unconditional love, given to us; that grace was the ingredient of our makeup that gave us value.

Knowing this, I developed a bit of a revelation about the messages I had been bombarded with from my mother, grandmother, three aunts, and countless neighbors in growing up Italian Catholic. I don't think they ever consciously linked "grace" with the daily realities of their lives because, as I heard it, they said *gratia* only for the good things, not the bad. I don't think it ever occurred to them to be thankful to God for pain, suffering, poverty, discomfort, depression, old age, and other perceived negatives.

Yet I think somehow that hearing how naturally these important women in my life discoursed with God made me subliminally conscious at a very early age of the relationship between grace and *gratia*. That's not to say I've lived my life consciously thanking God for the turmoil and traumas I've had to get through. Not at all. If I said that I could rightly be called a masochist. No, I'm sensible enough not to like pain, and honest enough to admit I'd like less of it. But, oh, what a teacher it has been. And oh, the mystery of it, especially when, almost shockingly, you feel joy from what pain has taught you, and from the depths of your heart, you utter a thanks be to God, finally learning, understanding, and accepting how grace and *gratia* are one and the same.

The outstanding spiritual writer and theologian, Henri Nouwen, expresses this wisdom from his personal experience of working with mentally handicapped people as pastor of Daybreak, a L'Arche Community in Toronto: "The deep truth is that our human suffering need not be an obstacle to the joy and peace we so desire, but can become, instead, the means *to* it," Father Nouwen writes in his *Life of the Beloved, Spiritual Living in a Secular World*.

> The great secret of the spiritual life, the life of the Beloved Sons and Daughters of God, is that everything we live, be it gladness or sadness, joy or pain, health or illness, can all be part of the journey towards the full realization of our humanity....The great spiritual call of the Beloved Children of God is to pull their brokenness away from the shadow of the curse and put it under the light of the blessing....

Just before reading this book, I had turned on my television set early one Sunday morning and the noted television preacher, Dr. Robert Schuller, was addressing a crowd. He was telling a story and it caught my attention. In summary, he was relating an experience he'd had during a visit to a palace in Teheran. It was being built or redecorated with mirrors. Every wall in the room was mirrored, and it was elegant indeed.

But then the master designer told the workmen to pick up hammers and smash the mirrors. They smashed and shattered the mirrors, and when they thought they were finished, the master told them to smash again and again, until the walls had turned completely into a mosaic of tiny mirrored pieces. And the effect was startling, incredibly lovely. With great satisfaction, the master explained what he had done and why. The mirrors had been "broken to be more beautiful," he said. And they were.

Dr. Schuller repeated that phrase over and over, "Broken to be more beautiful." In five words, he was passing on the meaning of pain for those who could open their ears to hear and their eyes to see.

It takes time, and, I guess you could call it practice-in-pain, before we can really grasp that mystery of how the traumas of our lives hold the power of transforming us into beauties. The poet Rainer Maria Rilke, in his *Letters To A Young Poet,* saw this mystery as so valid and so old that it has become an archetype:

> How should we be able to forget those ancient myths that are at the beginning of all peoples, the myths about dragons that at the last moment turn into princesses; perhaps all the dragons of our lives are princesses who are only waiting to see us once beautiful and brave.

To get to the place where we can recognize that the dragons are princesses-in-disguise, to use the poet's metaphor, is a tough and sometimes obscure path, most likely strewn with brambles. I also think it takes time, maybe even the better part of a lifetime. In a

book called *The Courage to Grow Old,* edited by Phillip
L. Berman, the venerable actress Rosemary DeCamp,
wrote:

> Our youth and most of our middle years are
> spent like the life of a dragonfly skimming the
> water; we seek the sun, flowers, and food, una-
> ware of the depths below or the sky above. We
> are glittering and beautiful, absorbed in self needs
> and all the lovely surfaces. As the years pass, the
> dragonfly disappears, hopefully replaced by a be-
> ing with enough curiosity to search the past, to
> ask the perennial questions: Who am I? How did
> I become what I seem to be....

And this lovely actress lets us in on where she has
arrived: "The long journey from the dragonfly to a 79-
year-old lady has been fascinating....Courage for the
crises was essential, but my overriding emotion is one
of profound gratitude; gratitude for what I have been
allowed to see, hear and feel." She has come to—
thanks be to God.

I can recall a day when I first became vividly aware
that I had not yet reached a wisdom that would help
me make sense of my pain. I had just discovered I was
pregnant again, for the sixth time, and I was devastat-
ed. Holding faithfully to the rules of my Catholic faith
which disallowed any artificial means of birth control, I
had gone through my 20s having a baby every two
years, married to an unstable man who lost his jobs
regularly. I felt as if God had crushed me with a cruel

hand when I found I was to have another child. For by this time, I knew the marriage was a shambles and that my young children needed to have a strong parent to support them and care for them. How could I be what they needed while I was physically and psychologically consumed with the responsibilities of yet another pregnancy?

To add to my agitation, the doctor, a general practitioner who had delivered my last baby, was no longer doing obstetrics. He suggested I go to a new doctor, a woman, who had just set up a practice in town. With an attitude problem that had me literally scowling, I went to Dr. Margaret MacKinnon.

Interestingly, she, too, was pregnant at the time, and so we had a rapport that is impossible for a mother-to-be to have with a man, even a very nice, understanding man. She sensed that I was in a bad emotional state, and while I was in her office, she showed me a book. It had been written by a woman doctor who had been one of her teachers at McGill Medical College in Canada. I don't remember the name of the doctor, who was by then deceased, or the name of the book, but I remember reading the introduction, and I never forgot her story.

This young woman had wanted to be a doctor at a time when very few women got accepted into medical school, but she was determined, and she made it. While she was there, she met a man and fell in love. He was not a doctor and resented the fact that she had to spend most of her time on studies and in the hospital, rather than on him.

He began to put pressure on her to leave, but she just couldn't give up the work she loved. Then one night they had gone out, and in a state of fatigue, she fell asleep. Feeling rejected and angry, he then gave her an ultimatum—him or medical school. It was the most agonizing decision she had ever had to make in her life, she wrote, but when it came to that crisis point, she did what she felt she had to do. She chose to be a doctor, an obstetrician.

A few years later a lovely pregnant young woman chose her to be her physician. When the doctor saw her name, she felt a stab of pain. This woman was now the wife of the man she had loved. As I sat in Dr. MacKinnon's office that August of 1962, reading what that doctor had written in her mature years about her life, I felt a connection. Tears came into my eyes when she told of the agony she felt when she delivered that baby, the one that should have been hers. And yet, she had also felt joy. She learned then that if she could get through such pain and feel such peace, she could get through anything that life would bring.

Her life did turn out to be a tough teacher. But apparently she had learned to turn her dragons into princesses. For what she said struck me with a force that impressed my soul and has never left. She said that if she had her life to live over, she would ask the Lord for one thing only: "Make it difficult."

Make it difficult! I had been seething internally at what I felt were the injustices and unfair burdens that the Lord had placed on me in my young life to date. I was shaking a fist at heaven, complaining that I had been given too much pain, too young. I was praying: "Make it easier!" And now I was reading about someone who, if she had to do it over again, had learned from her pain that she would ask, "make it difficult!" What did she know that I did not, I wondered? And so I began my quest to find out, wondering if the day would ever come when I could be so grateful for my difficult life that I could opt a second time for that blueprint.

Again, I think this not a state we reach easily or quickly. As far back as Plato, who died in Athens in 347 B.C., it was understood that wisdom took time to be fully savored, for as the great philosopher wrote, "The learners themselves do not know what is learned to advantage until the knowledge which is the result of learning has found a place in the soul of each."

I relate to that. Thinking back over my life, it almost startles me to reflect on incidents and realize that now, only now, do I really understand how these are just pieces God has been handing me right along so that I personally could design a mosaic of myself— promising, without coming out and telling me, that the more pieces, the more complexly colored, the more beautiful the final picture. But in the decades earlier, I sometimes felt jealous of the mystics who could welcome suffering, and, as Teilhard de Chardin wrote, find "the rapture of feeling that suffering is dissolving his being, drop by drop, and replacing it with God."

I think now of the preparatory lessons, mainly losses, some of which really stand out, like an incident back in the early 60s when I lost many "treasures" I had saved from my more youthful days. One of these dated back to the early 40s. I was a young teenager during World War II and had kept a careful scrapbook of headlines and stories while the war raged. It was my intention to one day pass on to my children an original historical document of that war. I also saved all the letters, written like poetry, that my wonderful Uncle Augie Sgambellone, then in the Coast Guard, sent me from the South Pacific.

There were other boxes, too, containing photos, early writing prizes, a few gifts from my mother and father, one of my golden brown curls cut from my hair when I was four, and my wedding gown. I had designed that garment and made it myself on my mother's old Singer sewing machine, and I had hoped one day to pass it on to a daughter.

But one day my husband took out all my personal treasures and burned them. I don't think I ever grasped what the lesson was he thought he was teaching me. It was cruelty, plain and simple.

Fortunately, just at that time I had stumbled upon a book written by Holy Cross Sister Madeleva Wolff, who for many years was president of St. Mary's College in Notre Dame, Indiana. The book had the strange title *The Relaxed Grasp*. In it, Sister Madeleva, who was also a poet, told how she learned that nothing in life is permanent. Loss is always the specter before us, she said, and the only way to cope with it and find peace is to have a "relaxed grasp" when it comes to clutching any of the treasures of this world.

Trying to hold on tight to things is the ultimate folly, the poet/nun was saying, because in the end we travel from this world with nothing in our hands. She indicated that loss was practice for the final trip. Learning to "relax" our grasp on material goods would help make the journey to our final destination more pleasant. The only treasure that merits a tight grasp is our final destination itself, she affirmed.

I have long lost her book, but her wisdom helped me to cope with every loss I've known for more than a quarter century. Bad enough to have lost so many personal things by fire, I one day had to face a similar loss from a flood. That was ten years ago, after I bought the house I now live in. I had no idea that my basement would get flooded from the record rains we were having in Connecticut that year. Everything stored in the basement was lost, including two irreplaceable boxes of magazines. These were publications I had saved over a period of some thirty years. Each contained an article or story that I had written.

In a sense, they were a record of my life, saved by me though long forgotten by anyone else. I mourned my loss, but not for too long, thanks in large part to Sister Madeleva, a nun I had never even met. She helped me in my struggle to relax my grasp on so many "goods" I would have chosen to have and hold on to, had the choice been mine. I would have never chosen to have my treasures burned, my basement flooded, a disastrous marriage, financial insecurity, ill health for my loved ones, and premature funerals. Sister Madeleva has long gone on her final trip. I'm sure she wasn't grasping any baggage that would chain her to the earth and hinder her vision of the promised treasure.

CHAPTER ELEVEN

THE PRIZE AFTER THE PAIN

Often when we are at a crisis point in life, in desperate need for help or solace, a gift is given to us in the form of a thought, sermon, book, or, most often, a person. Thanks be to God. We also have times when we get a personal revelation about ourselves that helps to strengthen our self-awareness and self-esteem, both of which are essential ingredients for coming to peace with pain.

This happened to me, when not long ago, I spent a weekend with my sister Rosemary at a conference called *Breakthroughs*. The leaders use a therapy called "Neurolinguistic Programming," defined as "the science of how the mind works," and a technique called "Time Line," the study of how "memories are stored and accessed in our mind and how this memory storage affects behavior." It sounded interesting.

The expectation with Time Line is that if one goes back subconsciously to a traumatic experience that has remained unresolved for your lifetime to date, you may be able to in a sense re-live that experience with new eyes and maturity and clear your past of this traumatic event. In so doing, you clear yourself of this lingering problem in the here and now.

The leader would select different emotions, like anger, shame, sadness, and guilt, and try to take us back in time subconsciously to identify first memories where these emotions were felt so that they could be "relived" now in a healing way and "cleared." I wasn't having much luck with subconscious "regression," but I did have an interesting recall when we focused on identifying our first memories of painful events.

I remembered a summer day when I was about four, back in my hometown of Albany, New York. In those days, milk trucks used to be driven by horses and I could again visualize the scene where a horse had fallen, hit by a car, his blood staining the street red. I cried in sadness and asked my mother if they would take the horse to the doctor. She told me, no, the horse would have to be shot.

I was, as one might expect, traumatized at the thought. But, contrary to what popular psychology might insist, I was not psychologically messed up. In fact, my reaction was not at all inward. It went outward. I felt the pain of that horse, and in a way this was my introduction to what it means to be concerned for another.

I then remembered a shocking incident that happened a few months later. My mother and godmother were in our kitchen and I was playing. I remember running to get something, and I tripped and fell against the hot water heater. This was an old-fashioned gas unit, where flames heated the water. When I fell, the flames leaped out, searing my right arm from wrist to elbow. I don't know who screamed louder, me, my mother, or my godmother.

We were poor, and in those days, like now, poor people never went to a doctor. My mother grabbed something called Unguentine, my godmother made a sling out of a ripped up pillow case, and that was the medical treatment for what was such a severe burn that the scars, like three flames, took over forty years to fade.

I was fascinated with that terrible wound, mostly because it seemed to get so much better in just a few days. In fact, by the fourth day I was doing so well that my mother let me go out to play in the back yard. The little boy who lived downstairs was already there. When he saw my arm in the sling, he came over to look. Then, with a gleeful smile, he dug the nails of his right hand into the burn wounds at the elbow and scratched the entire arm until blood poured out.

I ran upstairs crying, and my mother started to scream that I was going to get blood poisoning and lose my arm. Psychologists might have said that I would be scarred not only on my arm but in my head from something like this, but I wasn't. Again, I recall a sense of confidence that I would get better, and later I used to show off my terrible scars with pride.

That wasn't the last of my blows that year. The third and the worst was the death of my godfather Frank. We were always together and we loved each other dearly. He and my godmother had no children, and I was like their daughter. Because I was so young, my parents wouldn't let me near his coffin when he died, but I was with the funeral party from the church to the grave. I had so many questions about what death meant, and I was confused by the crying. All they told me was that God had taken my godfather to heaven.

That night after I had fallen asleep, I suddenly woke up. My sister Rosemary and I slept in a double bed. I was on the side next to the wall. I could see that she was sound asleep but I felt that someone was in the room and I looked up. There in the doorway of our bedroom stood my godfather. I could see him clearly because of the night light that was on in the hallway. He was staring at me and walked over to the bed. When he got to the side of the bed, he smiled at me, leaned over my sister, and put his arms out, as if to hug me or lift me.

I was suddenly frightened that he was going to take me away with him, and I called out to my mother. He still smiled at me. My mother came into the bedroom, turned on the light, and my godfather was gone. She was angry and didn't believe my story. She yelled at me that I was having a nightmare, turned off the light, and went back to bed.

I stayed awake for a long time thinking about this man I had so loved. No matter what my mother said, I knew this had not been a nightmare. My godfather had come to see me, and from that moment I knew that we don't really die. We stay alive in another way. I've thought about this night so many, many times in my life. I suppose there is a scientific explanation for why someone sees an apparition, particularly at a young age. If so, it just has never been important for me to investigate this. I know this vision was a heavenly gift from my godfather, to let me know that love lives forever.

Recent books like *The Spiritual Life of Children* by Robert Coles and *Child Spirit* by Sam Silverstein indeed affirm that many children have a rich spiritual life, though often lost, sadly, when they reach early adolescence. "Yet how young we are when we start wondering about it all, the nature of the journey and the final destination," writes Dr. Coles, an eminent Harvard psychiatrist. Certainly, that was my own personal experience.

At the *Breakthroughs* conference, though I had remembered those three incidents, my remembering did not achieve what the Time Line technique was purported to do. I didn't do any "clearing" when I went back in time. In fact, what I clearly understood from deep inside me was that the painful experiences all focused within the fourth year of my life had been the first stage toward getting me acquainted with the unexpected blows that life would deal me. Specifically they taught me something very important—that I could deal with pain, and that I would always survive.

It was good to have the revelation that early in life I had been given the grace I needed to learn from traumatic experiences. But in all honesty, in the future decades of my life, I didn't always think about grace when I was immersed in trauma. I would even get cynical at times when I read wise, cryptic statements meant to get me thinking positively. I even had one by James Russell Lowell pasted above my desk: "Mishaps are like knives that either serve us or cut us as we grasp them by the blade or the handle."

I wanted to believe that I was wise enough to pick up a knife by the handle, but that wasn't how it really happened. Life kept throwing the knives at me, blade first. But the truth is, and it sometimes surprised me, I kept surviving, actually with hope, smiles, and even joy. And now and then, I have had a light bulb go on, helping me see a little more clearly that if the world was relentless with its blows, God was generous with his grace.

One of those light bulbs went on a couple of years ago when I began to think about getting older and facing what is popularly known as a coming "transition." So I signed up for a session that could loosely be called "future focus," one of those intensive encounters with workbooks, pen, and paper. It was designed to get me to think about what I should do with the rest of my life.

First I had to find my "personal purpose." That wasn't as simple as it sounds. The workbook stated: "For every successful and satisfied human, the shaping of a life worth living starts with identifying and building on the purpose each of us was born to fulfill."

One couldn't argue with that. In fact I was reminded

of something attributed to Cardinal John Henry Newman who reportedly said that each of us has been given something to do in this life; we'll either find it and do it or we won't; in any case, we'll surely be told in the next world what it was we were supposed to do that we failed to do. That's a heavy statement.

Anyway, in the workbook I read that if we veer from the "path of purpose," we risk making decisions that will hurt us. We were instructed to list the six "best of times" and the six "worst of times" of our lives. It was explained that in the worst intervals we "experienced very poor results and very strong dissatisfaction."

I started thinking about some of the terrible times of my life—and there were many, like my mother's nervous breakdowns, the realization that my marriage was hopeless, being harassed on a job but unable to leave because I had to support my kids.

But, surprise! Those weren't times of poor results and great dissatisfaction for me. These were times when my performance actually excelled and when I made decisions that eventually brought great satisfaction. It was from the "worst of times" that I found the motivation and strength to go on, to rebuild. And so, as I sat there pencil in hand, I could think only of all the ways God had equipped me for my life. I even remembered a line from the *Meditations* of Marcus Aurelius that I used to reflect on rather cynically: "Nothing happens to anybody which he is not fitted by nature to bear." But now I sat there, wondering if I really been "fitted by nature" to bear what life would dish out to me.

I started to tally the blessings God had given me and realized that for every crisis and pain, I had received a resource to help me deal with it. Even the most searing torture, having two sons die, had its shining side: the beautiful years of mutual love with each of them.

I thought of my home, family, friends, my love of learning, my inborn energy, good health, attraction to laughter, my ability to write well enough to have made a living from this for myself and my children, and, way up there, my baptism which had made me a colleague of Jesus. I was overwhelmed with gratitude to my creator who had given me so much—even though it came wrapped in mystery. I must admit, I didn't fill in all the workbook's blank spaces on what I planned for the next twenty years. I just decided to play it really safe, staying where I had always been, in the inner circle of God's arms, trusting that there is where I will continue to find all I need to keep pursuing my ever-evolving purpose in life.

This doesn't mean we should sit back and wait for inspiration. The nuns used to put it to us squarely, "The Lord helps those who help themselves." Yes, the bottom line is that to find our purpose, to come to understand the meaning of life, and to achieve wisdom, we have to embark upon a lifelong course of learning.

I have interviewed many people who have had what Dr. Raymond Moody in his famous book *Life After Life* called "near-death" experiences. In all I have read and heard, people who live through such a remarkable experience come back to conciousness with an almost universal messasge. It is this: "What is most important while in this lifetime is to love and to *learn.*" I have reflected on this so often, and am I grateful that I have always had a love of learning, from science to philosophy. And yet, what is it that we are really to learn? Back in the 4th century B.C., Mencius, the follower of Confucius, wrote: "The end of learning is nothing but the search for the lost heart," and he believed this meant to "recover one's original nature" and preserve it.

I think there is truth in the words of that ancient wise man, for all learning should be pointed in one direction—to bring us to a universal love, which, of course, starts in the heart. But to get back our "lost heart," we have to confront and overcome the obstacles that keep us from loving. To do this, we have to learn the lesson of opposites—of cruelty/kindness, hot/cold, good/bad, yin/yang, pain/pleasure, white/black, love/hate, and on and on. For the mystery of creation is hidden in the hard fact that duality characterizes every aspect of life and that somehow we need to accept the mystery of opposites if we are ever to find our "lost heart." Only then will we be ready to grasp and say yes to Jesus' final commandment: "Love one another as I have loved you."

CHAPTER TWELVE

THANKS BE TO GOD

Not long ago I heard a talk by a very spiritual man named Abdul Aziz Said where he used the analogy of a dinner table to reflect on the duality in creation. The chairman of the Center for Cooperative Global Development and president of the Center for Mediterrean Studies, Mr. Said spoke at a conference with the theme, "A Revolution of Hope," put on by the Omega Institute, a holistic education center on an 80-acre campus in Rhinebeck, New York.

Mr. Said asked us to think of the guests we would invite to our table, and he listed those who should be on the list. He began with hope and suffering, for "they sit at the same table," and he mentioned others, like means and ends, power and authority, stability and change, self and other, creativity and discipline. "Action and vision knocked on the door, will and reason arrived late, as did joy and sadness," he said.

His point was "the whole world needs the *whole* world," and he brought us back to the table so we could "begin to connect...to feel what's going on." He asked, "What happens when we have hope without suffering...what happens when means disappear and ends remain?" He began to show us that hope without suffering is "an evening of illusion," that suffering without hope brings despair; that when all is means, "success is all that matters," and when we are "preoccupied with ends, we become fanatic." And so it went.

The metaphor of the table, he underscored, was to let us learn that we must be "generous enough to let *all* at the table." For this is the only way that "the inner and the outer become connected," the only way that we can become *one another.* And isn't this what the mystery of life is all about, to achieve the *oneness* that Jesus so urgently prayed for just before he left the table to go to the dreary garden?

> Father, may they may be one in us, as you are in me and I am in you....With me in them and you in me, may they be so completely one that the world will realize that it was you who sent me and I have loved them as much as you loved me (John 17:21).

If you hear this prayer and love it, then you have come to understand what the duality, or law-of-opposites, is all about. The design of creation is to get us to that wonderful unity where we are one with our neighbors. It is a message as old as earthly thought. Back in the 6th century B.C., Confucius "thought of people as related in 'one world—one family,' so that all shared a common destiny which was to be guided by the cultivation and extension of one's goodness to the service of mankind." Many of the mystics expressed the preexisting oneness of all things in God. Ralph Waldo Emerson wrote, "...within man is the soul of the whole; the wise silence; the universal beauty, to which every part and particle is equally related; the eternal One." Even scientist Albert Einstein spoke of our "essential oneness with the universe," he called the mystical "the sower of all true science," and he saw nobility in a "cosmic religious feeling."

The wonderful Dorothy Day, founder of the Catholic Worker movement, lived her life devoted to the "oneness" we all share with the One to whom we owe our origins. She wrote in *The Long Loneliness,* "These are the words of Christ, 'Call no man master for you are all brothers.' It is a revolutionary call...."

These are beautiful, rock bottom truths about creation itself and where we all fit into this grand scheme of the Creator whereby we are all *one,* intertwined by our common Source and our common Destiny. And yet, without some serious shakeups, we just can't go that distance to reach the unity required of true "brothers." We stay comfortably locked in our own skin, blocked from achieving what we were sent here to find and to give—in one word, love. We can't love others if we feel, or are, distant from them. Otherness and loving are intrinsically *one*—and God-like. And the great blessing is that we encounter so many people who have come through their own personal sorrows, softened enough to be ready to accept the revolutionary call for the brotherhood Jesus speaks of.

I was touched recently when I heard a talk by someone who had been shaped by pain, a woman who has come to a sudden and surprising fame—Clarissa Pinkola Estes, author of *Women Who Run With the Wolves*. The fairy tale ring in those words cannot be denied and what happened shortly after the appearance of her book, published by Ballantine in the fall of 1992, was like a fairy tale for Dr. Estes. Arriving originally with something of a thud, the book—clearly because of its originality and powerful theme—soon took off on a wild run of its own to become an almost instant best seller.

A Jungian analyst who calls herself a "contadora" or storyteller, Dr. Estes tells a story about her own past. "When I was a child, we lived in a strange part of the world. We didn't realize it was strange because we had never been anywhere else." She was born of Mexican parents but raised by an immigrant Hungarian couple in the steel mill territory of Indiana. They lived in tar paper shacks, in this impoverished, isolated place, and "Latinos were called the 'mud people' and 'beasts of the field' because we were not white." Because most of the people could not read or write, they "told their stories, singing their songs."

Then she went on, "this terrible, wonderful thing...happened when I was a child," and she shared a tale told to her by an old woman, about a hobo who had climbed over the walls of a zoo, causing the animals to bellow, and—could it be?—sing. When the people heard the sound of the animals singing, they were disturbed and confused, and they called the sheriff.

"He found this old man, playing his violin to the animals in the middle of the night, and the animals were crying back to him. Everyone said he was crazy.

"We [Clarissa and her two girl friends] were nine years old and thought he was the only sane one...to have the nerve to crawl over the wall of a zoo because he said he felt sorry for the animals—and so he played his violin for them."

She thought of this hobo man so often, playing for the animals, probably hungry, wearing ragged clothes and shoes. The police arrested him for trespassing. As for what he did, "Was it insanity—or an act of beauty?" she challenged.

"People said for nights after, that you could hear the animals baying...trying to bend the bars to get free... and something in us began to bend [our] bars," she said.

"That old man was open to do something so illogical" because he cared about suffering, and his act stirred them to feel the compassion he demonstrated. "He opened the hearts of three little girls who lived in the woods...I love him with a profound love." This man she never met stirred her to go on and "bend the bars" with courage, determination, and hope.

First she battled poverty, raising three children as a single parent earning money by baking bread, and then working her way through Loretto Heights College in Denver, eventually earning a doctorate.

Her personal story gave a special credence to the

message of her talk, which was to "open the door" of our hearts to be able to "feel for the world...be rich in sorrow" for the pain of people that is both personal and unseen and visible all around us, as in places like Bosnia and South Africa. "You have to have a strong stomach to tolerate the pain of the world," she said, urging everyone "to suture the wounds." She urged us to be united in our soul so that we could love with our hearts. Clearly it was from her own pain that she could take on the pain of others with much love.

It was the message of the gospels replayed, another translation of the plea of Jesus to be one with him and the Father, so as to be as intrinsically loving as they are. There's a catch, of course; the love-prize doesn't come free. First you have to be willing to accept that the passage to this unity and love is a crucifixion—in all the forms such pain can take in daily living, but one that comes with a happy new beginning, a resurrection.

This is the great leap—to get to the place where we can see affliction as a strong ingredient of God's love. The extraordinary Simone Weil, a French Jew who had come to the door of Roman Catholicism before her death at age 34 in 1943, made that leap. Something of a pilgrim, in search of truth and God as she confronted science, poverty, Nazism, and other perils of her times, she has now been given recognition as a "saint-philosopher-activist."

In her own words, she tells how she felt a gracious love in the midst of the tremendous pain she was suffering:

Christ himself came down and took possession of me.... I had never foreseen the possibility of that, of real contact, person to person, here below, between a human being and God.... Moreover, in this sudden possession by me of Christ, neither my senses nor my imagination had any part; I only felt in the midst of my suffering the presence of a love, like that which one can read in the smile on a beloved face.

In a commentary on Simone Weil's revelation, Princeton professor Diogenes Allen in *The Problem of Evil* writes:

We now come to the heart of the matter. Weil claims that in affliction we have the most perfect contact with the love of God that is possible for a human being in this life....Contact with his love can be joyous, even in the midst of suffering; for we can receive his gracious presence even in the midst of our distress. Finally, it is possible after such a presence is known for a person to be in distress and to recognize the very distress to be itself a contact with the love of God. This is not simply to recognize a gracious presence *through* yielding to suffering; it is to find the distress itself as the touch of his love....Sometimes through the universe of matter, God grips us very hard. That grip, though painful, is an indirect contact with his love.

Can we accept this? Can we believe in God's love when we get down so far that we would say with Gerard Manley Hopkins:

Wert thou my enemy, O thou my friend,
How wouldst thou worse, I wonder, than thou dost
Defeat me, thwart me?....
And then the poet pleas—
...O thou lord of life, send my roots *rain.*

I have prayed with Hopkins so many times, begging God to "send my roots *rain,*" never more earnestly than at the death of my sons. And my prayer was answered, so I could learn as Simone Weil did, that my affliction was the touch of God's love, even though I would have hoped that God's grip would be lighter.

What was most important to me after my son Peter died was to know that he was with God and happy, and I prayed for signs so I could know. Peter had seen his death as embarking on a journey to take him "home," and I accepted that, but being a mother, I wanted to know that he had reached his destination.

On Pentecost Sunday of 1991, two months after he died, I had spent much of the day with relatives, and we talked about and prayed a great deal for Peter. I prayed for the Holy Spirit to comfort me, but in a very specific way. I asked to receive just one more hug from my son. That may have sounded like a dumb request, but I've never hesitated to ask God for specific perks, and I've never complained if the answer was "no."

Anyway, that night I went to bed around 11, and as I was lying there praying, I was jolted by a loud bang against the wall behind my bed. I stayed put, eyes closed, thinking it was just a peculiar "house noise." A few minutes later, like a forceful slap against the outside wall of the house, the bang hit again. This time I opened my eyes, and I was startled by what I saw. I have a cathedral ceiling in my bedroom, and there, on the right side, where there is no possibility of outside light coming in through a window, was a glorious shower of light, like a myriad of flowing, shining bubbles.

At that moment, I was enveloped with a presence, from above my head to past my feet. It was as if I were covered with the most comforting, benevolent blanket that could be imagined. I had never felt such completeness. I smiled and said, "Thank you, Lord," for I knew that God had answered my prayer and given me the joy of one last hug from my son.

Some will scoff at this, believing that I have a wild imagination, emanating from wishful thinking. They are wrong. This was grace, God's gift of love to help me understand still more what I am to learn from my son's death.

The remarkable Helena Blavatsky, a mystic of the last century who founded the Theosophical Society—an organization devoted to brotherhood and altruism—maintained that we are not cut off from loved ones when they die. She wrote:

We are with those whom we have lost in material

form, and far, far nearer to them now, than when they were alive....For pure divine love is not merely the blossom of a human heart, but has its roots in eternity....Love beyond the grave, illusion though you may call it, has a magic and divine potency which reacts on the living....It will manifest in their dreams, and often in various events..., for love is a strong shield and is not limited by time and space.

With the death of a loved one, something amazing does happen to our understanding of time. Because we are still connected with the one we love, the boundaries between this world and the other are gone. Suddenly, life is no longer narrow and time-bound. With the boundaries gone, we begin to live in two worlds, experiencing an immensity of existence that is inexpressible. We are no longer limited by the confines of space and time. We begin to understand how truly we are all a part of eternity and God seems close, affirming what the mystic, Meister Eckhart, said: "There is no greater obstacle to union with God than time." This deepening sense of eternity is so wondrous that our response comes right from the heart, with a resounding "thank you." It is the prize after the pain.

We then see the world, the sky, the mountains and the trees, everything with new eyes, and new wonder. I found myself reflecting on what magnificent creatures we are, because we have eyes and ears and a brain. I had never focused on the miracle of eyes, which allow us to internalize the whole of creation by the simple act of looking. Imagine the mind of the Creator, who wanted to impress upon us our importance, and did this by letting us internalize the world!

When I worked at the college, I would often hear students saying that we humans are insignificant, that we are specks, that it didn't matter if we live or die. Then I tried to give them a spiritual approach to understanding life. Today I would simply tell them to look around. Everything they see is internalized; we have the sun, the moon, the stars, and other people, everything within us. In truth, we are universes. Could the Creator be any more explicit and loving in giving us importance? Doesn't this give clout to the promise of Jesus that even more "wonders await" us when we pass from this earth? I meditate on these lessons I have learned and can say now with joy that if it had to be pain that brought me to this place of peace, I can utter "fiat," and a prayer of thanks.

I didn't ask for my heart to be pummeled by life. I doubt if anyone would ask for this. Even Jesus in the garden asked to have the chalice of pain taken away. That's the human way. But God's way is different; it's the way of mystery. I think it has to be that way because of what's involved here, inviting us finite creatures to be one with the infinite. Somehow we don't automatically accept this invitation. We're too limited, too content with small, comfort-laden goals, with the here-and-now, with things we can touch and feel.

But all the while there is a mystery to be penetrated and a Source who wants us to opt for a permanent home. Enter the hurricane, the chaos, the disruption, the ways by which God disturbs us so as to shake sense into us. This is necessary. As the Jewish theologian, Martin Buber, expressed it, "All suffering prepares the soul for vision." When the vision intensifies and we begin to see what we were born for, then like a song from our pummeled but now open and peaceful hearts comes the aria: Thanks be to God.

EPILOGUE

I have a huge, very tall, gorgeous blue spruce in my yard. Every day in the ten years since I bought this property, I look out in the morning at this glorious, living gift of the Creator and I say thanks. I don't know who planted it or how many decades ago it emerged as a sapling from the earth, but it is now a treasure for the eyes to enjoy and the soul to relish.

One morning recently, I got up a bit earlier. The sun was rising, and when I looked out at that blue spruce, which stands like a cathedral in honor of the Lord, I stared for a moment in horror. The top third of the tree had changed color. No more blue, it was a dull shade of orange.

My first reaction was that something had been killing the tree and I had not noticed. Almost in a panic, I hurried to get dressed so I could go out and examine it more closely.

But then I walked into another room and looked out another window. The whole outdoors looked different. Everything had a glow about it. The sky was incredible, with shimmering sheets of silvery white clouds unfolding, as if paying homage to the great burning circle that had now emerged completely. The sun, which had been in hiding a lot in the late winter weeks preceding, was now reigning again.

I went back to look at my blue spruce. It was fully blue again. And then I realized that the orange I had seen had not been the sign of dying, but rather the sign of rebirth as the sun touched the tree, as if to alert it to the dawn of a new day.

I suddenly remembered another time more than twenty years ago when I lived in another place that had been saturated with rain for almost a month. I don't know if it was the gloom of the wetness or simply the circumstances of my life at that time, but I was at a very low point. I was working sixteen hours a day to support my children and life looked very bleak, nothing but non-stop work for a very long time.

This was a Saturday morning, and I had begun my usual housework and laundry. My youngest, Peter, then about five, had gone into the yard to play. Suddenly he rushed into the house, wonderment on his face. He excitedly told me I had to go out with him to see something.

I did. I stared. I saw nothing. I shrugged. Peter looked at me with a somewhat confused expression. "Mommy!" he exclaimed. "Look, it's a yellow day!"

I looked around and stared again, and this time I saw. The sun was shining and sharing its glow with everything in sight, glorious enough to awaken the response of wonder in a child.

Peter helped me that day to open my eyes to the miracle of a new day. He helped me almost instantly to abandon the emotional death I was entertaining and open my heart to the life around me. Yes, I was working hard and long, but it was for my children, and I was in the service of life—the yellow days of our years on earth. Instantly, I was out of the torment of my depression, and life was good again.

I remember other times when I was on the verge of despair and thought the bleakness of it was permanent. One time in particular was when I worked at a university and suddenly had a boss who was cold and on a power trip that left a lot of people destroyed in his path. I needed my job since I was the sole support of my children, and three of them were then in college. I felt betrayed and trapped as my work environment became more and more unbearable.

Then one day I got an unexpected phone call. It was a job offer to be the editor of a new newspaper starting up in another state, Connecticut. I took it and my life changed instantly for the better. If it hadn't been for that new, pain-inducing boss, I never would have left my safe university job to take on a risky, but much more rewarding one.

I know now, thanks to my faith, that life may break us, but God is there to put us back together. What I have learned is that so often when we feel we are in the depths, losing our luster and life—like a blue spruce turning orange—we are really at the end of a dark night, with a new redemptive day dawning. To see this, of course, requires an action on our part, but a simple one, really: the willingness to open our hearts.

FOOTNOTE

Shortly before this book went into production, there was a break in the case involving the murders of my son John and his wife Nancy. Montana's Lake Country Sheriff called me from 2,500 miles away to tell me: "We've got the person we think killed your son and daughter-in-law."

The news he gave me stunned me. The suspected killer, he said, is the 18-year-old son of the couple from whom John and Nancy bought their house in January of 1993.

As the story started getting pieced together, it was unbelievable. The boy is a first-year student at a Quaker college in Oregon. I am told that he started talking about killing some people to a fellow student at the college. This person, in turn, reported what he had said to the campus security officer, who then went to the police.

By the time I was called, the officers from the Criminal Investigation Bureau who had been assigned to the case, had gathered considerable information from the suspect. The young man revealed that he had a gun and had left it with a friend in Kalispell, Montana, when he left to go to George Fox College in Oregon. The police retrieved the gun and ballistic tests confirmed that it was, indeed, the murder weapon. Within a few days, the young man was in jail without bail. His parents hired an attorney and he entered a "not guilty" plea. From here on the legal story is left "to be continued."

But what can be pieced together is searingly painful. This is apparently a kid everybody calls nice. He was a good student in high school. His parents are fundamentalist Christians, "very religious" people according to the Sheriff. And their son went to Christian schools.

The question remains *why?* What happened? If my son and daughter-in-law died at his hands, why did he do it? As of this writing, investigators have yet to come up with a motive.

Many have asked me how I feel about the apprehension of this suspect. And I answer, simply and honestly, "incredibly sad."

I am learning so much. I remember once in an ethics class when I was getting my Masters degree and the subject of capital punishment came up, I adamantly opposed it. But then, in all honesty, I had to add, "But if someone raped and murdered my daughter, I'd say, 'kill the bum.'"

Now, though the scenario is slightly different, I face the actuality of that crime. And where do I stand? To my own surprise, now that we may be moving toward a closure on this tragedy, I feel no anger, only sadness, and certainly, I remain opposed to the death penalty. So many lives have been blackened by this shadow. There is only one response, sadness.

Resources

Note that these resources are in the order in which they appear in the book.

John Leinenweber, *Be Friends of God, Spiritual Readings From Gregory the Great*, Cowley Publications, 1990.

Jesus Christ Superstar, Leeds Music Corporation, 1970.

Pope John XXIII, *Journal of a Soul*, McGraw-Hill, 1965.

Percy Knauth, *A Season in Hell*, Harper & Row, 1976.

Charles Eliot Norton, translator, *The Divine Comedy of Dante Alighieri*, The Encyclopedia Brittanica, 1952.

Ernest Hemingway, *A Farewell to Arms*, Scribners, 1987.

Sister Joan Puls, *Seek Treasures in Small Fields*, Twenty-Third Publications, 1993.

Faith Baldwin quote from Anne Wilson Schaef, *Meditations for Women Who Do Too Much*, HarperSanFrancisco, 1991.

H.A. Overstreet, *The Mature Wind*, W.W. Norton & Co., 1949.

Kierkegaard and Oscar Wilde quotes from *The Choice Is Always Ours, The Classic Anthology on the Spiritual Way*, edited by Dorothy Berkley Phillips, Elizabeth Boyden Howes and Lucille M. Nixon, Harper & Row, 1989.

Max Cleland, *Strong At the Broken Places*, Cherokee, 1980.

Patricia Neal, *As I Am*, Simon & Schuster, 1988.

Ludwig Born quote from *Meditations for Women Who Do Too Much*.

The Fellowship of Merry Christians, Carl Samra, founder, P.O. Box 660, Kalamazoo, MI 49005-0668.

Andre Dubus, *Broken Vessels*, D.R. Godine, 1991.

Diane Berger, *We Heard the Angels of Madness, One Family's Struggle With Manic Depression*, Morrow, 1991.

John Welch, *When Gods Die, An Introduction to John of the Cross*, Paulist Press, 1990.

Gerard Manley Hopkins, *Poems and Prose*, with an introduction and notes by W.H. Gardner, Penguin Books, 1985.

Chad Walsh, *Behold the Glory*, Harper, 1955.

Teilhard de Chardin, *Building the Earth*, Dimension Books, 1965.

Henri J.M. Nouwen, *Life of the Beloved, Spiritual Living in a Secular World*, Crossroad, 1992.

Rainer Maria Rilke, *Letters to a Young Poet*, W.W. Norton, 1962.

The Courage to Grow Old, edited by Phillip L. Berman, Ballantine, 1989.

Dialogues of Plato, Jowett translation, Washington Square Press, 1963.

Marcus Aurelius and His Times, The Transition from Paganism to Christianity, Classics Club edition, Walter J. Black, 1945.

Raymond A. Moody, *Life After Life*, with an introduction by Elisabeth Kübler-Ross, Mockingbird Books, 1975.

Ch'u Chai and Winberg Chai, *Confucianism*, Barron's Educational Series, 1973.

Ralph Waldo Emerson, *Essays*, National Home Library Foundation, 1932.

Dorothy Day, *The Long Loneliness*, Harper & Row, 1952.

Clarissa Pinkola Estes, *Women Who Run With the Wolves*, Ballantine, 1992.

The Problem of Evil, edited by Marilyn McCord Adams and Robert Merihew, Oxford University Press, 1990.

Simone Petrement, *Simone Weil*, Pantheon, 1976.

Sylvia Cranston, *HBP, The Extraordinary Life and Influence of Helena Petrovna Blavatsky, The Founder of Modern Theosophy,* J.P. Tarcher/Putnam Books, 1993.

Meister Eckhart, Teacher and Preacher, edited by Bernard McGinn, Paulist Press, 1986.